Mindful Social Marketing

How Authenticity and Generosity are Transforming Marketing

By Janet Fouts

For information contact janet@janetfouts.com

Cover design by Elke Weiss

ISBN: 978-1-4951-9032-2

First Edition: October 2015

DEDICATION

I could never do what I do without the love and support of my family. Even with the crazy hours, frequent travel for speaking and training and my obsession with all my digital gadgetry, they've held true through it all and given me nothing but love and support. CJ and Mike, I love you and am endlessly grateful for you.

FOREWORD

By Bryan Kramer

When Janet mentioned she was writing a book focusing on "mindful marketing," I was eager to read how she'd approach the topic. She builds upon a concept close to my heart - one I've written upon as well - so I knew Janet's vision would throw a fresh, new spin on the work I covered in my books: *There is No B2B or B2C: It's Human to Human* and *Shareology: How Sharing is Powering the Human Economy.*

Mindful marketing starts from the notion that the advertising industry has become increasingly cluttered with marketing messages - so much so that consumers have developed ways of filtering them out. To capture their attention you need to create content that resonates with your target audience and drives engagement. Marketers must move away from a standardized approach and be more human in connecting with prospects. And that means that we need to be mindful in our methodology.

I've previously outlined a few mindful marketing tactics, which involve:

- Taking a Customer-Centric Approach: Align your company's interests with those of society.
- Asking Thoughtful Questions: Focus on issues that truly matter to your audience.

- Establishing a Mindful Experience: Be in the moment.
- Shifting Your Thinking: Respond to a constantly changing marketplace.
- Sending the Message: Deliver through channels that are most likely to reach your audience.

Janet runs with these concepts by pointing out how mindful marketing means being genuine, being generous and listening more than speaking. In the book she demonstrates how, ith a mindful mind-set, you can:

- Slow down a frenetic pace to be more productive;
- Leave distance between the anxious reactions of others and gain a more solid perspective on the world around you;
- Train your attention to align with what your target audience is drawn to;
- Learn to be a better listener so you can be a better communicator;
- React more professionally and less frantically to criticism; and,
- Relish in a sense of accomplishment instead of dealing with a stressful work environment.

I particularly liked Janet's discussion about listening with intent and developing a strategy to actually do something with what you hear. She offers a few tips that will benefit marketers in any industry.

Trending News: Your social listening will reveal the hot topics that your target audience is talking about online. Provide additional information that offers value in the form of an answer to their question or a solution to their problem.

Supplementary Information: What you're hearing from your potential customers can transition over into related topics where you can provide additional details.

Social Listening Rules: Technology is a valuable source to establish "rules" that identify topics - which can then be used to create content. Show off your generosity by giving up valuable information that your target audience can use *now.*

Another point that fascinates me about Janet's perspective is the importance she places on getting an entire enterprise's team on board with mindful marketing. A customer-centric approach to marketing is everyone's job and even the biggest brands are implementing employee advocacy initiatives. They're encouraging personnel to spread the word about the brand, talk to customers and otherwise engage with people. It's not a new concept; it's just one that's been diluted as more of your target audience goes online to search for information. There was a time when organizations thought that the voice of the company should come from the C-Level executives; today's consumers want to hear from the daily grinders.

A company's employees have the knowledge and experience - in both the industry *and* with their employer. There can be no better resource to generate goodwill than the people who deal with it every day. Your team has enormous capacity to motivate loyalty, impact social sentiment and move a company forward. Cultivate them by offering support and training in social media strategy to give them a role in your marketing strategy.

A final point that you will really learn and enjoy is the importance of having a well-defined content calendar for your mindful marketing strategy. You develop your content around thoughtful, generous advice, but you need a strategy in place to ensure it's delivered in the right place, at the right time. You'll end up doing a lot of wheel spinning if you don't have an established plan for getting your material out. A content calendar will help you sort out what you have, categorize it by topic and channel - and map it out to the right people at the right time.

I could go on to detail all the powerful points and valuable advice in this book, but Janet's book speaks for itself in terms of the benefits you'll gain from her insight. Mindfulness is the future of marketing, which is effective because it aligns business objectives with socially responsible interests. Marketers looking to tap into these benefits will avoid the common hassles of wheel-spinning and clutter to establish a meaningful connection with the target audience.

CONTENTS

INTRODUCTION

"The future is always beginning now." - Mark Strand

I work with an incredible range of companies, from nonprofits and agile start-ups to huge Fortune 500 corporations and everything in between.

This book came about because I was frustrated with working like mad and feeling like I could never get on top of all the things I had on my plate. I had no time to enjoy my life, my family, my friends, and I felt the same thing from the people in the companies I consulted with.

I wrote this book because I realized: we all need to be **more** *responsive* and **less** *reactive* to things that come up on and offline. That means deciding when something has to be responded to immediately and when it needs to settle a little bit before we respond to it.

We are inundated with message after message full of drivel that clearly no one, not even the author, really means or cares about. It is totally ineffective messaging driven out of the need to produce, rather than an interest in the intended reader.

Where is the authenticity, the desire to connect and impact someone one-on-one?

With the fire-hose of information on the internet, how does a marketer stay sane?

How can we be effective, enjoy our jobs and have real communication with the people we want to connect with?

How did social marketing get so far from being social and human?

If you're already using mindfulness practices in your life, this book will give you new insight on how to bring your practice into marketing, as well as providing tested social media marketing techniques that will help pull it all together.

If you're a marketer who feels overwhelmed by all the new roles, tools and strategies getting thrown at you, mindfulness will increase your efficiency and help you be happier at your job. You'll also learn some new strategies for social media marketing along the way.

Bottom line, Mindful Social Marketing will teach you how to use mindful business practices to be more focused, present, effective and happy at your job, and truly reach people, not targets.

I bring 20-plus years of experience as a digital marketer to teach you how you really can be a mindful and effective social marketer.

This is going to be great! Let's get to work.

CHAPTER ONE

What is mindfulness all about?

"Mindfulness means paying attention in a particular way, on purpose, in the present moment, without judgment." - Jon Kabat-Zinn

Being mindful is about being present -right here, right now. Not thinking about the future, or the past. You're not thinking about what you're going to have for dinner, the mistake you made on that spreadsheet yesterday, or the response to that email you just sent. Being mindful removes the baggage that we carry with us into meetings, conversations, presentations or any situation, really.

Being in this exact moment without those distractions leads to a better focus on the issue at hand and deeper insights into what you are doing *now*. For marketers, it helps us see issues more clearly and brings the focus to what matters.

It's about acceptance
People are who they are. To communicate or work with them, we have to start by accepting who they are. If someone disagrees with our position on a topic, we don't have to take it personally.

We can accept that we have differing opinions and not take it personally. If we make a mistake, we can accept that it is simply a mistake. We all make them, but we don't have to dwell on them and beat ourselves up for it.

We accept that the traffic is bad and call ahead to let people know we will be late; without feeling the need to blame anyone or rage about the road conditions. What good will that do anyone?

We accept that it's raining and find something else to do on a Saturday - maybe sitting on the front porch with a good book and listening to the rain, instead of railing against it. Why waste that energy?

We accept that not everyone agrees with everything we say or do and understand that that contrast, between what *we* think and what *they* think, makes life interesting!

It's about kindness
Being kind to yourself and others allows you to speak from a more centered place and remember that we are all in this together. Other people face the same challenges and want the same things for themselves as we do. The practice of "loving kindness", also known as "Metta", is one of the foundations of mindfulness practice. Metta practice is a sincere wish for the welfare and genuine happiness of all beings, without exception. Some say that feels frivolous, or "woo woo", but the effect of practicing Metta can be dramatic.

A study in 2014 at Yale and Michigan State Universities (Kang, Gray & Dovido, 2014) discovered that, compared to a control group, those who undertook 6 weeks of loving-kindness meditation training significantly decreased their biases against minorities.

In a study conducted at Stanford University by Cendri A. Hutcherson, Emma M. Seppala, and James J. Gross, one short period of loving-kindness meditation increased the participants' acceptance of and feelings of social connectedness with strangers.

Ninety-three participants who meditated for no more than 30 minutes a day (if at all) were trained in brief meditation exercises. Participants began with the instruction to close their eyes, relax, and take deep breaths. They were then instructed to imagine two loved ones standing to either side of them and sending their love.

After 4 minutes, participants were told to open their eyes and redirect these feelings of love and compassion toward a photo of a stranger appearing in the center of a computer screen. Participants repeated a series of phrases designed to bring attention to the other, and to wish them health, happiness, and well-being. They were then asked how connected, similar, and positive they felt towards the people in the photos.

Even that one session of loving kindness practice was enough to impact their feelings of both explicit and implicit positivity toward strangers. The results suggest that simple kindness practice can increase positive emotions towards others and that we can, indeed, train ourselves to feel connected with and act kindly toward a relative stranger.

A study at the University of Massachusetts Medical School asked frequent migraine sufferers to attend one 20-minute session of Metta practice. After the session, the participants reported a 33% decrease in pain and a 43% decrease in emotional tension.

It's about noticing

The practice of noticing puts you in the present moment and makes you more sensitive to context and perspective.

When was the last time you sat in a board meeting with a dozen people, none of whom were listening to the presentation being made? Then someone asked a question, and you had no clue what to say? What if you put down your notebook or your smartphone and focused your attention on the presentation and the reactions of other people in the room?

You may be surprised at the details you've missed. Being impatient by nature, I've found this trying at times. But, as I put mindfulness more and more into practice in my work, I've found that I'm more aware of subtle shifts in behavior, indicating that people notice that I'm noticing and listening to what they have to say. Sometimes they seem a bit relieved or even grateful for the attention. How sad is it that it is exceptional to be not only listened to, but also heard?

Likewise, the act of stopping to actively notice has saved me time and energy when managing social media crises. Noticing the details around an issue before you respond to it can affect the action you take. The perfect response or solution to a problem may be staring you right in the face, if you only stop to see it. Observing that people are beginning to talk about a problem with your product or spotting a subtle shift in language can give you the advantage of early knowledge and the time to formulate an intelligent and appropriate response.

It's about curiosity
Being curious without judgment heals a lot of small problems before they become larger ones. Pursue your curiosity. Why is it this way? Why do you feel that way? How could we do this differently? Ask questions, before judging and reacting without enough information.

When you are building community through your social media networks, you will need to know a lot about what the people you want in your community talk about. What are their needs and pain-points? What do they talk about that could help you strike up a conversation? What is driving them?

Often, we are in such a rush to get to the next thing and the next thing that we don't even slow down to ask the right questions. Without accurate information, we make knee-jerk decisions we regret and spend more time fixing them than we ever would have if we'd simply asked and made an informed decision in the first place.

It's about responding rather than reacting
There's a huge difference between reacting to a comment and responding to it. All it takes is a few seconds of quiet and calm before you respond. A snappy reaction may send the wrong message or fan smoldering embers into flames. A thoughtful response may reward you with the appreciation of the recipient.

To respond, you need information. You may need to take a breath and stop and think about it, so you don't let emotion carry you somewhere you don't want to be. Give yourself and the other person the respect of responding thoughtfully.

It's about intention
What's in your heart? What do you mean to say? Think about that before you create a new message. What is the intent behind it? Strategy and intention surely go hand-in-hand in marketing. A clear intention and a defined strategy to get there can make a world of difference in the success of your marketing efforts.

What will mindfulness do for me?
There have been many studies done on the benefits of mindfulness. One such study at the University of North Carolina-

Chapel Hill found a correlation between mindfulness practice and better relationships in couples. Couples reported improved closeness, acceptance of one another, autonomy, and general relationship satisfaction.

Another study of 70 primary care physicians in Rochester, New York involved mindfulness training, including guided meditation, awareness, and appreciative inquiry exercises. The physicians were guided through exercises to increase intra-personal self-awareness and mindful movement exercises as well. The study demonstrated the effectiveness of this training in reducing stress, anger, depression, and burnout. The physicians showed improvements in empathy and self-compassion as well. The skills they acquired in their training appeared to lower reactivity to stressful events and allowed them to show greater resilience in adversity.

The biggest benefit to you from even a small amount of mindfulness practice is likely to be reduced stress levels. Dr. Jon Kabat-Zinn, Ph.D. explains his Mindfulness Based Stress Reduction (MBSR) in this video: [1] filmed at Google in 2007.

You can expect mindfulness to bring a calmer, more focused approach to many aspects of your life.

- Things seem to slow down, and you are able to get more done.

- You get a little distance from the frenetic reactions of others and a more grounded perspective on what is going on around you.

---

[1] MBSR Video – Jon Kabat-Zinn http://j.mp/1JjMwlq

- You can train your own attention, and by setting that as an example, the attention of those around you.

- You'll be a better listener, and thereby more effective at communicating your message to the world.

- You'll be less reactive to criticism and more in control of your emotions.

- You will stop sweating things you cannot change and see stress significantly reduced.

- You will be more productive because you'll be better focused.

- You'll get your dopamine from the pleasure of a job well done, instead of the unpleasant rush of a stressful job situation.

How can I be more mindful and still get my work done?
Some seem to think that mindfulness means you're sitting around in the lotus position and humming for a large part of your day. Sure, some meditators do actually meditate for long periods of their day. Others simply take a few moments a day to check in with themselves. Are they in the moment or is their mind off somewhere else?

Tech entrepreneurs like Loic Le Meur, Evan Williams, and Arianna Huffington are very public about their mindfulness practice and the advantages it brings them in their work. See Loic's talk, "Meditation - from seeing it as bullshit to daily practice" [2] at

---

[2] Meditation – from seeing it as bullshit to daily practice
http://j.mp/1ir2THq

Wisdom 2.0 as he reveals his experience with meditation.

Meditation can significantly impact your life with just a few minutes of practice a day. Simply training yourself to be present - really listening in that meeting, really concentrating on writing that email or taking that phone call - will make things easier to accomplish. Because you're here, and you're focused.

The multitasking myth
We've been told for much of our lives that the ability to multitask is key to being productive. Neuroscience has shown that isn't true at all. When we think we're multitasking, we're actually mini-tasking.

Our minds flit back and forth from one thing to the other so fast that we don't even realize it, but we are actually doing each task one at a time in fast succession. Often in our day-to-day work, we end up doing a lot of things mindlessly while we rush towards our goals. We could be much more effective and efficient if we just did one thing at a time instead of trying to do it all at once!

Think about a typical business meeting. As people enter the room, they're thinking about the agenda, their next meeting, their kid's school field trip, or the angry customer they will need to call later. Is their boss there yet? What's for lunch? Are they going to have the right answers to the questions that might come up? What documents did they need to read before this? The list goes on and on, doesn't it?

Some people open a laptop or pull out a tablet and pretend to take notes. But the whole time they're checking email, playing games, or posting to Facebook. Others are doodling or making lists of things they need to do after the meeting. They're not present, much less mindful.

In The Organized Mind [3], Neuroscientist Daniel Levitin tells us that even though we think we are getting a lot done when multitasking, it makes us less efficient. Multitasking has been found to increase our production of the hormones cortisol and adrenaline, which can over-stimulate your brain and cause mental fog or confused thinking. Multitasking also creates dopamine, effectively rewarding the brain for losing focus and constantly searching for more stimulation. In short, it feels good and we want more!

Glen Wilson of Gresham College in London calls this phenomenon "infomania." His study of volunteers found that trying to focus on a task when bombarded with emails and phone calls can reduce IQ by as much as 10 percent. I'm guessing that's not a surprise to you. Is it?

Psychologist Daniel Goleman, the author of **Focus: the Hidden Driver of Excellence,** says: *"We have been seduced by distraction ... We are being pulled away from paying attention to the things that enrich our lives."*

To test the multi-tasking myth, try uni-tasking. This is quite literally doing only one task at a time. See what a difference it makes to focus, finish, and then move on to the next thing. Once you can train yourself to do this all, or even most, of the time, you'll see a dramatic improvement in your ability to get things done. You'll have more time in your day.

I'm a fan of the Pomodoro Technique to help with uni-tasking. The concept is simple. Set up a time frame in which you will work on

---

[3] The Organized Mind http://j.mp/1OJMwT5

only one task. These are usually short bursts of time during which you focus on just that one thing without distraction - 25 or 30 minutes is the norm. Then stop and take a break for 5 minutes. Get up and stretch, walk around, or just breathe and relax for 5 minutes before going back in for another session.

Break time is just as important as the focused time when you're working. It gives your brain the ability to process what you've done and also to rest and be sharp for the next round.

I used an app on my desktop called Pomodoro Timer when writing this book and it was an immense help. I worked for 25 minutes, then got up and took a break for 5, then went back to work. Every 4 sessions, I took a slightly longer break of 15 minutes and did something unrelated - like going for a short walk, playing with the dogs, or working in the garden. Give it a try, and let me know how it works for you.

Listen
You know those people who sit down with you to chat and you feel as though they are hanging on every word? It may not be love, it may just be that they are paying attention. When people pay attention to what we are saying, when they really listen, we feel revered and respected. We generally leave the conversation feeling good about ourselves and the other person. Think about how much more productive that makes us.

Simply listening with full attention is a wonderful way to have a deep and meaningful conversation with someone, and it doesn't matter if it's a business or a personal one. It also doesn't matter if it is a Twitter conversation or an email exchange. The same applies to any method of communication.

Be present. Listen without rushing to judgment and pause before you respond. You'll find you make fewer mistakes in your messages, and less impulsive and inaccurate responses. Try it next time you have a meeting and you'll see what I mean. More on listening skills in Chapter 5.

Pay attention

As you go through your day, make a mental note of when your attention wanders or you are multitasking and, just for a moment, stop. Direct your thoughts to your breath. Take one deep breath and then release it slowly. That's all you need to do. Allow yourself that tiny amount of time to re-focus on the task at hand.

Notice if you sense irritation for no reason, or react to some small annoyance with an out of proportion response. Again, allow yourself a moment to re-focus. Breathing is an easy way to do this, to help you break the frenzy and simply settle. Take a breath in through your nose, counting to 4. Hold it for a count of 2. Breathe out through your mouth to a count of 4, emptying your lungs completely. That's it. How did that feel? If you are *really* irritated, do this 2-3 times until you feel your heartbeat slowing down and you are calmer.

Use this technique whenever you find yourself feeling harried, stressed, or just needing to settle before you take action.

Mindful meetings

When you call a meeting, whether online or in person, have a clear agenda. Start the meeting with a moment of quiet. Everyone puts their electronics and notebooks down and simply sits quietly for 15-30 seconds, leaving all the distractions they brought with them from their day behind. No need to chant or even meditate. Simply recognize that you are all there, present for the meeting and ready to go. Then pay attention. Look at the person talking and listen. Hear them out and then speak. Don't allow distractions like ringing cell phones to happen. Be fully present.

At the end of the meeting, take a moment to recognize the people in the room and their contributions to the success of the meeting, without any judgment. You don't have to tell them this aloud if you don't feel the need, just make a mental note to yourself, recognizing the value that everyone brings to the table.

Focus in a crisis

Crisis management is easier when you're present and focused. Avoiding chasing distractions is easier if you can teach yourself to be truly present in that moment, and that's a whole lot easier if you have been practicing being mindful before you need it in a crisis!

When you are focused, you're listening to what the other person has to say and responding, rather than reacting. You take a few seconds to clearly see what's going on. You make fewer mistakes. You have time to consider the other person and issues involved, then respond with kindness and compassion - and a whole lot less panic. When you're present, it's easier to stay grounded and not freak out!

When we are dealing with social media marketing, we sometimes see what appear to be small bumps in the road bloom into full-on catastrophe in a matter of minutes. Generally, we can look back afterwards and see what it was that started the whole mess. We realize there was a moment we could have handled the situation differently, to a different outcome. It's possible that we were running so fast, we really didn't see the cliff looming ahead of us.

Unless you are in a life or death situation, you can almost always take the time to look before you leap. Take a breath and analyze the situation. Does action need to be taken now? Are you the right person to manage it? Then, formulate your plan to resolve it if need be.

Experienced marketers know this: bad things happen. Being prepared is part of mindfulness. too. It's how you respond to the issue that makes all the difference. Putting processes in place for the most common occurrences before you need them, as well as training your team on how and when to put the wheels into action, can make a huge difference. When you are prepared with the tools and the focus brought by mindfulness, you will be ready for anything.

Social media distractions

Social media can be an extremely difficult environment in which to uni-task. Even staying on just one network at a time can be a challenge. Remaining focused is rewarding and worth the effort. Concentrate on your goals and re-read the posts you create before you hit send. We'll go much more into this in Chapter 2. Suffice it to say that being focused on one network at a time and one post at a time will avoid many silly mistakes made in a rush.

Do I have to meditate?

That's a common question, and the easy answer is no. The more complicated answer is: "You don't have to, but you will find it immensely useful if you do." Go watch Loic Le Meur's video again and see what I mean.

Mindfulness is about being present and aware. You don't have to meditate to be successful at mindfulness. I will tell you that it helps, and if you start with meditating just 10-15 minutes a day, you will see a surprising impact. In the resources section of Mindfulsocialmarketing.com, you'll find links to explain how meditation can help you and many ways to bring it into your life without joining a monastery. This includes some wonderful websites and apps that make meditating easily understandable and bring a sense of wholeness to your life.

I'm not going to tell you that you have to spread incense all around your office, chant a mantra, and spend a lot of time in complicated Yoga poses. That's not what being mindful is about. It's also not about your chosen faith. This is not specific to any religion. Mindfulness is simply about taking the time to be here, right now. To be in this moment and not a million other places all at once. However, should you choose to pretzel yourself into Yoga positions in your office, I'm not going to be judgy about it.

In Real Happiness at Work: Meditations for Accomplishment, Achievement, and Peace [4], Sharon Salzberg says, *"Through meditation, we can come to understand work problems as a potential source of achieving greater clarity, rather than as obstacles without redeeming value, and begin to recognize the true potential of the challenges that work brings our way."*

If you are considering meditation, her book is an excellent read with some exercises to help you get started meditating in the workplace without feeling weird about it...

If you don't want to meditate, you could just get started by identifying your mindful moments. Take one minute to stop and notice what you're doing right now. Are you present in this moment, or thinking about that recipe your friend gave you? Thinking about how you're going to get through your day? Wondering if reading this book will make you late for a meeting? Being present is a discipline, just like mindfulness, that you can practice every day to help you be more focused, efficient, and happier.

---

[4] Real Happiness at Work: Meditations for Accomplishment, Achievement, and Peace http://j.mp/1mSKPsG

Time to be present

My friend Liva Judic, a mindfulness teacher, passed on a great idea. She said, "Set a timer on your watch, on your phone, or on your computer to go off at a random time each day. When that alarm goes off, stop and ask yourself the question, 'Am I present or not?'". This will help you understand how often you're focused, or not. Such a simple practice can help you see more clearly the need to stop, breathe and be *here*.

Another great idea to try? Blink. Just blink and remind yourself, for the millisecond that it takes you to do so, that you're here, you're focused, and you're paying attention to what you're doing right now. Or you're not. Notice that too.

Being present all the time is not something that happens overnight, if ever. Over time, and with practice, you'll begin to notice less and less that you are distracted. You'll be focused, more efficient and happier because you feel at one with what you're doing.

When brands are mindful

The number of brands who have a mindful approach to their marketing is growing by leaps and bounds, and it's not as unusual a list as you may think. Google, General Mills, Etsy, LinkedIn, Indiegogo, Goldman Sachs, and the Huffington Post are just the tip of the iceberg. These businesses see the benefits of having a less stressed, more focused, happier and healthy workforce.

Keurig Green Mountain

At Keurig Green Mountain in Vermont, founder and chairman Robert Stiller incorporated mindfulness into the corporate culture. There is an on-site meditation room. They offer classes and retreats at the Center for Mindful Learning in nearby Burlington, VT.

This company is focused on the good of not only their staff, but the community around them as well. Keurig Green Mountain donates corporate funds to support the Burlington school district's wellness and resiliency program, benefitting teachers and students by teaching them how to manage stress through courses and retreats.

Patagonia

Patagonia, a leading maker of outdoor gear and apparel, is known for their green approach to business. They even produced a documentary film called 'Worn Wear' to convince their customers to buy less stuff. Ads proclaim "Don't buy this jacket" to encourage consumers to reuse and repair their clothing, rather than buying new. This attitude shows deep understanding of their market, and their reverence for the earth. The campaign launched in 2011 and sales grew by 40% in the following 2 years. Maybe people really did want to make a conscious, intent-driven investment in clothing built to last. Those ads are still making news today, in 2015.

"For companies to transform on a larger scale, individual leaders must transform." - Casey Sheahan, former CEO of Patagonia

Facebook

We've all seen flame wars and shaming on Facebook. Brands can be attacked here with impunity because it's become part of the culture of the users. Within Facebook, however, it's a very different story. Facebook brings in teachers on meditation and mindfulness and encourages staff to take the teachings to heart.

Peter Deng, Director of Product at Facebook was on the stage at Wisdom 2.0 in 2014 and spoke about his process for getting organized with his to-do lists and calendar, setting intentions for the day so he can clear his mind for the tasks ahead. This focus on intention in day-to-day life is extremely helpful in a hectic work environment. Here's the video of his talk: "Applied Mindfulness: Peter Deng".[5]

Facebook is taking a mindful approach to the online experience of its users, too. I attended the 5th annual Facebook Compassion Research Day in 2015, and it was an eye-opening look into how Facebook supports and assists users to be good netizens.

Facebook's Director of Engineering, Arturo Bejar, and the "Compassion Team" are working on fine-tuning the user interaction on Facebook to help people resolve conflicts with empathy, combat bullying, and even assist those who may be experiencing depression or having thoughts of suicide.

A Facebook user who sees a friend in distress can find resources on the site to learn how to help, or the user can ask Facebook to review a post and Facebook's support team will respond in a high-touch way to help the at-risk person get the help they need in a compassionate way.

This team hosts the annual "Compassion Research Day" at Facebook, where they share partnerships created with youth organizations, emotional intelligence projects, suicide prevention, and the science of happiness among others. Learn more and view recorded broadcasts of the event at https://www.facebook.com/compassion.

Aetna
In 2010, 239 Aetna employees participated in a study called "Mind-Body Stress Reduction in the Workplace", a stress management program based on the principles and practices of

---

[5] Applied Mindfulness: Peter Deng http://j.mp/1MAMfIN

mindfulness meditation. Ninety-six employees were randomly assigned to mindfulness-based classes, 90 were randomly assigned to therapeutic yoga classes, and 53 were randomly assigned to the control group.

Since the study concluded, Aetna has expanded the availability of the programs to all Aetna employees nationwide and some their customers. Employees report a 28% decrease in stress levels, a 20% improvement in sleep quality, and 19% reduction in pain.

"We have seen first-hand how these mind-body programs have helped our employees deal with stress more effectively and help them achieve better overall health," said Elease Wright, head of Human Resources at Aetna, in a 2012 news release. *"We are excited to offer these programs to more Aetna employees and are confident that our customers that implement the mind-body programs will see similar results with their employees and lower costs associated with stress."*

Aetna's CEO, Mark T. Bertolini, recently gave approximately 5,700 of his lowest paid employees a 33% raise. He stated at an economics conference that, *"Corporations can make the investment in their communities and their employees, and we can improve the middle class as a result."*

ON CBS news, Bertolini said, *"If we're going to invest in our people to get them engaged every day, we have to reduce their stress levels, we have to pay them fairly, we have to allow them to live their lives fully so that when they're taking care of other people, they don't have all that other baggage with them"*.

It is clear that in this age of rising health costs and levels of stress in corporate America, embracing mindfulness is simply good business. I highly recommend David Gelles's "Mindful Work" [6] as inspiration on bringing mindfulness programs into your workplace and for several more stories of corporations incorporating mindfulness into corporate culture.

Today's workforce isn't satisfied with just a job. They want a sense of purpose, they want fulfillment and happiness.

It should be obvious by now that mindfulness is beneficial to us personally, at home and at work. The corporations listed here are just a few of the ones who clearly see the benefit. Now we need to bring that mindset into our marketing, too.

A mindful approach to marketing brings humanity to our messaging. It offers a way for us to connect on a personal level and create deeper relationships with our users and our markets. It opens many more doors to communication, and isn't that what we are supposed to be doing here? Communicating?

Mindfulness allows us to take control of our environment and the many situations that pop up from time to time. Instead of rushing around putting out fires we really can take a moment to breathe, consider, then choose to act. We may not be able to control the flood of information that inundates our world, but we can control how we respond to it.

****

Do this
Think about when you've had that mindful moment in your day. How does it feel? Set an alert on your phone, then take one minute to be mindful. If you're at your desk, take it a little at a

---

[6] Mindful Work http://j.mp/1MI6Do7

time and incorporate mindful moments throughout your day. Now see if that makes your day just one iota less hectic.

Mindful Moment

Mindfulness is not about meditating all day. It's not about religion or political affiliation. It's about focused attention and getting more done with less stress. Doesn't that sound good right now?

CHAPTER TWO

How is Social Marketing Different?

"I love social media. I love the connectivity it provides, the creativity it allows, and the breathtaking wealth of information we all have at our fingertips because of it." - Galit Breen, Kindness Wins

Social marketing is the same as traditional marketing, isn't it? It's all marketing, right? Not really. Social marketing is, by definition, social. This means it requires interaction with humans, preferably one-on-one. It's about people, connections, relationships, education, generosity, and sharing a long time before it's about "marketing" a product or service. Social marketing requires a human voice in order to really reach the market, engage them, and encourage them to take action.

Traditional marketing in print, TV, radio, etc. is often called "push marketing", or "interruption marketing." It's all about getting the message in front of the target market. The strategy is to get that message in front of as many eyeballs as possible, as often as possible; in hopes that it will stick and the buyer will remember it when the time comes to make a buying decision. There is little or no interaction with the decision-maker directly, and certainly no relationship established at this stage. We can only guess (or hope) who the viewer is and what their interests are, based on demographics given us by the media channel.

"Finding new ways, more clever ways to interrupt people doesn't work," - Seth Godin

As opposed to interruption marketing, social media marketing is often called "attraction marketing". We use what we know about the needs and interests of our market to attract them to us with content that is particularly valuable or entertaining to them. Interaction and data analysis on social networks allows us to get to know so much more about our customer. We have a tremendous opportunity to truly listen to and understand the people we want to reach, if we simply take that time.

The major difference between traditional marketing and social marketing is this: it's about people, not markets.

When we make the effort to focus mindfully, listen, and pay attention, we can learn about our markets' needs and desires, and engage in conversations that can turn cold or non-existent leads to warm leads. Doesn't everyone loathe making cold calls? Doesn't everyone loathe getting a cold call? The sales team can significantly reduce the necessity for cold calls if there is relationship building going on for them in social media.

Even with this clear advantage over traditional means, it's been very hard for brands to make the shift from handing all their marketing over to an agency, expecting them to produce marketing materials with little or no input from the brand, to actively engaging in their own marketing.

It's common to see a brand starting out on social networks by producing piles of posts, apparently just to hear themselves talk or to fill enough space to raise their visibility. They're bringing the same old mindless tactics, "yell and sell", to the wrong party. If that's what you want to do, get a billboard next to a bullet train track and call it a day.

Pause for a moment and think about the person who is seeing all these jargon-filled posts stuffed with the "right" keywords. Put yourself in their shoes.

Would you follow you? Does it feel like a fire-hose of noise? Does it feel like everything is automated, and there isn't a real human behind it? Does someone answer when a question is asked on a social network?

That may be marketing, but it's not social marketing. It's more like a banner ad or a TV commercial. We're going to skim over it and go somewhere more interesting. When was the last time you clicked on a banner ad? Do you even see them anymore?

A mindless post results in a mindless or negative response, if any at all. Mostly it's just the un-follow or block button, at least in my case. I don't have time in my day for thoughtless marketing noise.

Today's consumer expects to get information for free and indeed, in large part, they can. Even if it's not the spec sheet on your newest product, they gather the data they need to make a purchase decision online, through social connections and friends. We stand in the aisle in front of a coveted product and Google it to find the best price and reviews before we buy.

In 2014, an e-commerce analytics site, MineWhat.com, quoted research showing that 81% of consumers research online before buying.

According to the 2014 State of B2B Procurement study from the Acquity Group:

- 94% of B2B buyers report that they conduct some form of online research before purchasing a business product.
- 37% of B2B buyers who conduct research through a supplier's website feel it's the most helpful tool for research.
- 44% of respondents have researched company products on a smartphone or tablet in the past year

It's clear that research by both B2B (Business to Business) and B2C (Business to Consumer) customers is happening online, and trust in peers is a deciding factor.

"The "social generation" is heavily connected to brands and one another, aiding in the fluidity of conversation between business and consumer, and also peer-to-peer interaction" -Elite Daily

Elite Daily reported on the findings of a study[7] with 1300 millennials.

- 1% said a compelling ad would influence a purchase decision.
- 33% review blogs before making a purchase.
- 3% said they used TV news or print media as a resource.
- 43% ranked authenticity over content when consuming news.
- 62% said they are more likely to become a loyal customer with a brand who engages them on social media.
- 75% said they expect a brand to give back to society in some way.

---

[7] Millenial study http://j.mp/1iHODut

There is no question that millennials expect more interaction and they do their homework. It is also clear that they are leading a sea change in how all demographics do their research online. As we become more social the lines between demographics mix.

As users start exploring for information the demographics they engage with changes too. My social networks are made up of a blend of Boomers, Millennials, and Generations X, Y and Z, and it isn't always easy to tell through social conversations which are which. As we talk to each other, we share the latest technologies, apps, strategies and news, and everyone is moving rapidly toward the same path as found in Elite Daily's study!

Clearly content is still king
You can spend money on ads to get in front of buyers, but conversation and engagement are equally important. Sharing content related to your product has to be part of your marketing, of course, but it's only the start. Once you get buyers to the content, you want to build that relationship. You need to be having conversations and developing trust in the brand as a whole. Through these conversations, you are creating dedicated brand evangelists to help you reach more deeply into your market, expanding the recognition of the products and the brand.

Whether you're a mom and pop shop or a Fortune 500 corporation, creating the content necessary to keep the flow of information, entertainment, and marketing moving through the social channels is essential.

******

Do this
Survey some of your customer base and see how they get their information. What networks are they using and how can you

create a presence there that will be beneficial to them?

Mindful Moment

The days of "Yell and Sell" are dwindling. Now is the time for you to think about your customers not as a target market, but as humans who want to interact with you and your brand. When it comes to the end of the day, we are all people with the same needs and desires, whether we are customers or marketers.

CHAPTER THREE

Employee Advocacy

"An employee's motivation is a direct result of the sum of interactions with his or her manager." - Bob Nelson

Employee advocacy seems surprisingly new to big brands. This is when you encourage your team to help get the message out, talk to customers, and otherwise interact to support the company they love. It is, however, by no means a new concept; businesses have done this for ages. At some point, corporations decided it was better to leave certain areas of business to the "professionals" and backed away from allowing employees speak for the company, letting agencies or consultants do it for them.

Now, I'm not saying all consultants or agencies are bad. (Heck, I own an agency and I'm a consultant!) What I am saying is that employees who are well informed and empowered have tremendous capacity to move your company forward, and you ignore them at your peril. Be grateful for the value of the knowledge bank in your workforce. Partner with employees to support them and train them in social media strategy and compliance, to enable them to have a role in corporate social marketing.

I asked author and social marketing strategist Ted Rubin to give us an example of employee advocacy and its *Return on Relationship™*. (#RonR)

"What's the fastest way to devolve from the old "agency" way of thinking to social communication? Empower those who work for you to create conversation and represent your brand-especially those who have a customer service or customer-facing role. If they build it, service it or sell it, they're in a perfect position to communicate with your audience in a way that humanizes your brand, but only if you let them.

"Many companies that are fearful of social media put muzzles on their employees to control the social conversation. However, if you're going to have a social presence at all, just the opposite needs to happen.

"Apple's "Genius Bar," is a perfect example. Check it out for yourself. Go into any Apple store and count the number of blue shirts milling about in the retail space. It's astonishing-and each one is an Apple genius whose sole purpose is to communicate with customers, answer questions and share knowledge one-on-one. However, you don't get a hard sell. The emphasis is on providing helpful information. In doing so, each employee puts a "face" on the Apple brand and turns a shopping excursion into a human experience.

"The great thing is; you don't have to hire a zillion blue-shirts to stand around your company store to do the same thing for your brand. With a little guidance, your current employees can be blue-shirts for you in social circles.

The key word here is guidance! This includes having a written social media policy for your employees, going over it with them, and involving them in the process. Your employees can be your best advocates and a natural extension of your brand that gives you much better Return on Relationship™ than advertising ever could-but you need to switch your thinking by opening up your internal communications first.

"Sit down and talk to your employees about how they can communicate your company mission and values. Open up a dialog. Get their opinions. Involve them in the process of creating a social media policy so they feel empowered to spread the word about you within the right framework. But make sure that you do not overcomplicate the process and make them feel they are under a microscope. Opening internal lines of communication and building healthy employer-employee relationships is the first step. The next is figuring out how to train them to communicate externally.

"The short of all this is that in today's digital age, you can't afford to try to control your company's brand. You need to learn to let go and become involved in the conversation already going on about you in the social space-and let your employees help you. Otherwise, the cost in market share is steep because competitors that "get it" are already out there eating your lunch.

"Now, I'm not saying you should let go of all the reins; there must be some structure and planning involved. However, a good social strategy MUST involve your employees. Give them some leeway. Educate them about your core values, and about what's appropriate to share in social circles. Train them to be your brand evangelists and you'll be amazed at the resulting Return on Relationship!"

I couldn't say it better myself. Be sure to visit Ted's website at TedRubin.com for more insight. He's an amazing font of information, and he really walks his talk.

The combined reach of your employees often outshines that of the marketing department alone, and their original and unique voices add authenticity to the brand image. There are many ways to encourage your employees to take a role in the company's success. Often, staff shies away from talking about the company online because they're afraid of getting in trouble for saying the wrong thing. This is an easy fix. Give them some guidance. Create a corporate social media policy - not to stifle employees, but to enable them.

Social media policy
People are much more comfortable engaging for the company if they know the guidelines and have some examples to go by. Social media policies let everyone know what the rules of engagement are. Depending on what industry you are in, there may be compliance issues. Or, maybe the company is about to go public and there will be a "dark period" beforehand. People need to know this.

Intel's famous social media policy[8] is incredibly short, and to the point. It's written in plain language for all to understand:

Disclose
Your honesty-or dishonesty-will be quickly noticed in the social media environment. Please represent Intel ethically and with integrity.

Protect
Make sure all that transparency doesn't violate Intel's confidentiality or legal guidelines for commercial speech-or your own privacy. Remember, if you're online, you're on the record-everything on the Internet is public and searchable. What you write is ultimately your responsibility.

Use Common Sense
Perception is reality and in online social networks, the lines between public and private, personal and professional, are blurred. Just by identifying yourself as an Intel employee, you are creating perceptions about your expertise and about Intel. Do us all proud.

I've paraphrased here, but you can find a copy of their social media policy, as well as many others, to use as a model for your own in the resources section of the website.

Basic components of a social media policy
Here's a short list of elements you should include in your social media policy. Even if you're a one or two person shop, go through these and answer each one as an exercise to clarify

---

[8] Intel social media policy http://j.mp/1ir9txy

your intentions.

- Why are you using social media and what do you expect to gain from it? Ask yourself some hard questions about why you really want to use social media. "We have to have a Facebook" is not an answer.

- What networks are you using and how will you use them? Make lists of the networks you think you want to use and why those particular networks are a good fit. This is not going to be every social network on the planet, but we'll get to that discovery phase later in this book.

- Who's in charge? There should be one person or a team of people who are responsible for finding the answers within the company for anything that comes up on social. If an employee doesn't have the answer, they can simply respond to a comment on a social network and say they will find out and pass it to the proper person. Be SURE to follow through with this or your employee is left swinging in the wind.

- Who should post? Is there a social media team responsible for the posts on the company pages? Let people know who they are and how to contact them.

- What content is shareable? As marketing and PR develop messaging they want to get out, figure out how to disseminate this to the employees in a way that makes it easy for them to share. This may be through a newsletter or an intranet.

- What content should be avoided? If there are corporate secrets or hot button items you don't want brought up, be sure everyone knows about it. This may seem basic or something everyone should know but it's important. Trust me, I've seen this many times.

- What branding should be used? This can be a biggie. If people want to share something and they don't have the right logo or photo, they'll make something up. Be sure everyone has access to the brand messaging, mission, logos, photos of the CEO and product shots that are approved for use. This way, all branding and imagery of your company and products is consistent and high-quality.

- How do you expect employees to conduct themselves? A tiny amount of awareness training can go a long way here. Teach people what they should and should not say. If they post on a social network promoting the company's product, they are required to disclose they work for the company. They can do so in a profile or with a simple disclosure. "I work for company X, all opinions are my own" is one common form.

- How do you want to handle negative comments? It can be hurtful for an employee to be told on their own social network that the product you make sucks! Create a protocol to help them manage this effectively. This is where compassion comes into play. Putting themselves in the shoes of the consumer can be greatly helpful in managing and resolving an issue.

It is really cool to see employees actively engaging on the company social media accounts. Not just "liking" every single post (though this is a strategy to keep visible in the news feeds on Facebook!), but rather taking an interested role in answering questions about the product and sharing information relevant to the problem it solves. Employees frequently build their own community of practice around their special interests. Help them do this and you'll see a generous return on their loyalty.

Why let employees Tweet?

Twitter and all the other social networks worldwide are opportunities for you and your employees to stay up to date on current events, as well as friends and family. Professional development can take many forms, including scanning social networks for information to share with their community of practice. Don't ignore an opportunity to learn or restrict your employees from doing it either. Support them and train them in best practices, if necessary.

HR and talent attraction

If your employees are happily engaging on social networks, they send a message to the world that your company is a good place to work for. Seeing that smart, happy and engaging people work there makes everyone else want to work there, too! Let them know of new positions and how to support HR.

****

Do this

Create a social media policy and go over it with your employees. They should sign off on it so they know what to do. Then, create a way to keep everyone informed and give them access to the information they need to support the company on social media appropriately.

Mindful Moment

People are going to use social networks on their own anyway, so why not take a centered approach and give them the tools and knowledge they need to do it in a way that benefits everyone? We all want to feel valued and useful beyond just doing our job. Invest in your team and they will return the favor.

CHAPTER FOUR

Set yourself up for social media success

"Social media is not about the exploitation of technology but service to community."
- Simon Mainwaring

When choosing social media networks, we tend to fixate on the networks that we like, or that someone told us we should like. Perhaps we have a lot of friends on Facebook, so we naturally want to run our business on Facebook as well. This is not the best way to make a business decision. The correct choice of network depends on many factors. It's important to remember that social media is not about the networks in and of themselves. Networks come and go. Rules change, best practices change, people move on.

Social media is social: it's about the people, not the networks.

Check your intentions
Have you established the markets you want to reach? Do you

know what you're going to talk about? Are you clear on the roles you and your team are going to play? Do you have a pile of resources and ideas to share? No? Don't worry, this chapter will help.

Do some searches
What social platforms are people using to have conversations about the topics you want to discuss? Instead of trying to boil the ocean, define your niche market verticals. Find out on which networks those people are participating. Then, be there. Don't worry about being everywhere.

You can NEVER be active on every social network and still get your job done. Why waste your energy and passion on a network where users are not interested in what you have to offer? Focus is key. Trying to be on every network is the antithesis of mindful social marketing.

As we evolved our brand from online community to web development, then to online education and, finally, back to community (now called social media), we've responded to the market we serve and kept mostly ahead of the game because we are always listening. This has allowed us to change with the times and survive two recessions in one of the toughest markets for tech companies in the country, Silicon Valley. Because we listen.

But enough about us. Let's get back to how you decide which social networks to use.

To set yourself up for social media success, you want to shift your thinking from a focus on how you're going to sell your product and how truly great it is to a more mindful approach based on the needs and dreams of your market. To do that, spend some time listening to them and getting to know who they are.

Get to know your market:
- What dreams do they have for their businesses?
- What do they need?
- What problems can you help them with?
- Where do they get their information?
- What are their other interests?
- What resources do they trust?
- How do they prefer to communicate online?
- Do they use your competitors? Why?
- What will you do for them that is different?
- Are there secondary markets?
- How can you speak to the secondary markets?

Answer these questions about the people who care about the same issues as you. Walk through each of the above points individually to define one or more market niches. Don't discount secondary markets - they will be a source for content, leads, and sales.

For example:
I made up a company called "Two Dog Leash" (there actually is one, but I have no association with them), the be-all end-all of dog leashes when you have two dogs to walk at the same time. How much marketing can you do on social media just about a two dog leash?

First, think about the issues these dog owners care about and become a helpful resource for them. What other interests or concerns are common to people with two dogs?

- Toys
- Treats
- Dry food? Wet food? People food?
- Safety
- Fireworks
- Kids and dogs
- Introducing a new dog
- Aging
- Puppy training
- Traveling with a dog
- Pet sitting
- Getting your dog used to the cat

As you can see, the opportunities are almost endless. With a little more thought, we could fill pages with ideas, couldn't we? Take some time to consider all the aspects your niche is interested in and make lists - lots of lists. Talk to existing customers and your sales teams. What appeals to them and how can you best relate to them?

Mind mapping tools can be helpful in defining your market niches. The goal is to get into the head of your market and make as exhaustive a list of discussion topics as you can.

The way I use mind-mapping tools may be a little different than other people; for me, it's a virtual whiteboard, except it's better because I can move things around and reorganize. As you go through the process below, write down every idea you think of. You may not find content for all of them but don't worry about that now. Just let the ideas flow and get them on the board. You don't have to use each of them, but by making a complete list, you may uncover some niches that you would have otherwise overlooked. As you list ideas, your picture of your market may well evolve and morph, and new discoveries will emerge.

Back to our example of Two Dog Leash:
Write down the things that might concern your market. After writing down everything you can think of, group your ideas into categories - housing, feeding, medical care, training, traveling, etc. You'll start to see your perspective evolving and a big picture developing. That big picture will help you to define one or multiple niches of information and avenues that you can target. This is just a top-level way to get a handle on what topics you could potentially discuss.

Here's a simple example mind map for Two Dog Leash:
As you can see, you quickly get an organized diagram of ideas for relevant topics you can address. We will cover how to source information in the content section. Suffice it to say that with mindful attention to the needs of your market, you'll have no shortage of ways to connect with them.

Where is your market?

Once you define these various topics of discussion, you'll have a picture of a fairly broad niche and maybe even some segments of that niche to focus on. You're going to need to find out where people in that niche participate online.

What social networks do they use? Do they comment on blogs? Are they interested in tweeting? Do they have videos? Perform some searches. Use the listening tools listed in the resources section of the website to find out where people are having those conversations.

Once you identify those networks on which your niches are participating, you know which networks you can focus on. This will not necessarily be the same old networks you're used to, or even your favorite new networks.

Now you can create a plan. Decide which of the networks are best suited to you. Think about which ones will make the biggest difference. It could be any number of sites. Remember, you don't have to be on them all at once, or even ever.

What we're doing is getting a big picture and identifying where our market is having conversations. Then, we can give more thought to how best to communicate with them. We can learn how to curate content from those networks and share it on other networks.

Take some benchmarks

You're going to want to understand how to measure whether or not you're being successful. Look at your sales level: how many phone calls are coming in the door and the number of sales-related emails you receive. What other metrics are you looking to improve through your social media outreach?

If you already have a lot of social media accounts, write down your numbers. How many retweets did you get? How about comments and shares? It's not just about the number of fans and followers. Followers are no good to you unless they DO something. That something might be as simple as sharing your content with a friend or associate who needs you.

Look at some of the social media measurement tools in the resources section of the website to find ways to take those metrics, and do it before you take any more steps into social media. It's crucially important to establish a starting point so you can see the progress you're making, and then take that progress and celebrate it with your team. If you've never had a social media presence, that's okay. Start at zero - just write it down.

At first, progress will be slow. But, as things grow and you start to expand, you'll start to see more success. That's when you know that taking a mindful approach to social media marketing has helped your business. Do not expect this to happen overnight. Give yourself time to build a real network. That could easily take a few months, but the network you build will give you much more return on your investment than one created without intention.

Now that you know your market and where they engage, you're set up with a solid footing to go forward. Starting out prepared with a comprehensive knowledge of your niches will make it much easier to market mindfully to people who want to hear from you on the networks you choose.

Where should you be?

If it seems like there are too many social platforms, don't worry. You don't have to be on every one to succeed. In fact, it would be a waste of your time and energy if you were! Remember: we are about focus here. Stay focused on the networks and communities in which you feel most comfortable and which are the best fit for you and the way you communicate, as well as your market.

If you like blogging and longer-form content, then, cool! Stick to the platforms that thrive on longer discussions.

If you're excited about creating how-to videos, video blogging or live-steam video - go for it! If video scares you to death, you don't have to go there right now, if ever. You may decide to hire someone or use someone on your team who likes to be in front of the camera.

If you love to share information and curate links to content your market will love, look for the networks where you can share quickly and easily, adding your own take on it as you go.

To succeed on any social network, you need to be comfortable with that network and its particular style of communication. If you're not, and it's a super-important network for you to be on, find someone who is. Use those listening tools to decide if this is the right network for your market first, and then decide if you need help or training to make it work for you.

How does your market consume?
Your market may consume content primarily on the desktop, a mobile device, or in print. If it's video, they may be streaming their mobile device to their television or another screen. Each of these formats need to be taken into consideration when creating your plan.

About time
Social media marketing is a lot of work and is most definitely not free - especially in the early phase, when you are starting out and doing all of the groundwork. Setting up your accounts, finding or creating content, and learning the ropes will be a lot of work, and it's setting the stage for your success. As you get accustomed to your networks, you'll find you spend less time working behind the scenes and more time engaging with people. Be patient here and cut yourself a little slack as you learn.

It's not going to happen overnight. But, within a few months, you should be able to settle into a rhythm that works and see the amount of time spent struggling with new tools and creating or sourcing great content significantly reduced.

The keys to not wasting time on social media are: staying focused on your reasons for being there in the first place, having the training you need to execute your social strategy, and showing strength of character by not chasing every shiny new toy that passes by. (That's a hard one for me!)

Social media can be insanely distracting. If you are on your business Facebook page and you see a notification from your college roommate - keep your focus on business. Do what you need to do and get off, so you can get the rest of your work done. Don't watch that cat video until you get home.

In Peter Bregman's 18 Minutes- Find Your Focus, Master Distraction and Get the Right Things Done, [9]Peter talks about the trap of momentum - how you can be running so fast in one direction that you simply can't put on the brakes. You know how that is? It happens all the time in social media. You get rolling sharing news, then you see a post you just have to comment on. You share with a friend or co-worker and, before you know it, you've killed an hour. Or maybe a day! Peter offers a lot of great ideas in his book for managing your time and getting more done. It's a great read and I recommend you take the time to read or listen to it.

My advice is: wherever you find yourself, step back and take a 10,000 foot look at where you are. Right now. Do you really need to be doing what you're doing? Are you locked into moving forward on this network just for the sake of doing something?

Take a breath. Get up and go for a walk. Break the flow for a moment. Then, decide if you really need to be doing what you're doing or if it's a procrastination tactic to keep from doing something else more important.

---

[9] 18 Minutes http://j.mp/1LqU3oH

If you have a hard time managing the time you work on social media (or anything else, for that matter), I've found the Pomodoro method to be effective.

Blocking out a few times a day to monitor your accounts should be sufficient in most cases. You do not need to have your accounts open 24/7, unless you are using them for customer service or something like that.

Tools for social media management
There are a number of tools that can help you be more efficient with social media management. Some are definitely more mindful than others in their approach.

Browse the resources section and look for tools that suit the way you want to work. Some of them, like SproutSocial,[10] allow you to manage your social profiles, schedule posting to multiple networks, and even import RSS feeds so you can curate content right from their dashboard. They'll also give you reporting on what is working and what is not, so you can fine-tune your messaging to best effect.

I'm not a huge fan of automated direct messages and pushing messaging into the laps of your network. I much prefer thoughtful scheduling to share intentionally. We will talk about this a lot more in the content chapter. Suffice it to say that scheduling is OK as a tool, especially if it frees you up to be fully present at the right time.

---

[10] SproutSocial http://j.mp/1NG9oSt

Be kind to you

Kindness and compassion for yourself and others is an important element of mindfulness. As you are learning all this - the social media networks, the tools, the processes - cut yourself some slack. If this is all new to you and/or your team, allot a little extra time and avoid self-criticism. Evaluation is important, but in good time. Enjoy the thrill of those first social media wins. Celebrate successes and you will, over time, be confident that you have the tools and skills to get it done.

It may be useful to attend training on the various platforms through a training consultant or a course like the ones we offer on MindfulSocialMarketing.com. Lynda.com is another resource for learning the basics on most networks.

If you are a beginner, accept the beginner's mindset. You aren't supposed to know it all yet. Enjoy the exploration phase and try to minimize self-criticism or over-evaluation of yourself and your team.

******

Do this

Make a mind map of everything you can think of about your product, business and brand, then group your ideas to identify the niche or niches that seem to be a good fit. Do some searches to see where people are having conversations that are relevant to you and your market. Learn what kind of language they use, what their voice is, and how things are phrased on the different networks. Use that knowledge to craft your messaging and choose your networks.

Mindful Moment

Setting yourself up for success requires organization, strategy, and a thoughtful and compassionate approach to your market. Put yourself in their shoes instead of looking at things only from your side of the table. Think about what they want, not what you want to give them. This change in perspective can make all the difference in the world.

CHAPTER FIVE

Listening with Intent

"Leaders who are great listeners are often terrific at uncovering and putting in place strategies and plans that have a big impact" ~Sir Richard Branson

Now we have an idea of where our niche "lives" on social networks, so let's talk more about strategic social media listening. There is a lot of talk about social media listening, and how important it is for brand monitoring, customer service, professional development, and competitive analysis. Unfortunately, there isn't a lot of information on exactly how to listen or what to do with what you hear. This chapter is here to help you with that.

Being a good listener is the key to a good conversation. It's a basic rule you learn early on. Listen, pause, think, respond. Listen some more.

Attentiveness in a business situation is so important that corporations send teams to listening skills training. Yet, in the lightning-fast medium of social networking, we can get lazy and forget all we've learned. We jump to conclusions without truly listening to what the other person is saying. We make assumptions and confusion ensues. This especially happens with networks like Twitter, where we try to cram as much information as possible into one tweet of 140 characters and there is an implied sense of urgency to respond quickly.

Listen, Think, Respond

If you don't listen carefully, messages are easily misunderstood. When this happens online, a simple mis-statement can be wildly misconstrued, and damage control needs to be activated. To avoid that, take time to listen.

Listening requires focus

We can read the text or hear the words, but to comprehend the meaning we must pay attention - not only to the story, but to it's context and the language used to convey it.

In other words, the subtext is often as important as the message itself. When you look at a series of messages on a micro-blogging site, they may be totally out of context, and you'll need to go back and re-construct the context to see what is really being said.

When you have a face-to-face conversation, you have the other person's body language and facial expressions to take into consideration. You gather intelligence from what you assume (wrongly or rightly) from the person's sex, race, attire, and age. The conversation happens in real time, so the context is easy to see.

When you see a conversation online, it may not have a date attached to it. The thread of the conversation may cross social networks or take days to roll out.

Even if it's a deep conversation with lots of threads online, you can decipher what is going on by following the comments back to the source.

Keep it simple

Once you have an idea of what people are talking about, phrase your social media messaging as humanly as possible. In Bryan Kramer's There is No B2B or B2C: It's Human to Human,[11] Bryan says, *"Human beings are innately complex yet strive for simplicity. It's the simplicity of our favorite communicators, brands and products that make us fall in love with them, because we get what they're saying. It takes a lot of hard work to make something so complex look so easy. Some call it brilliance, but perhaps we should call it speaking human."*

Customers want to be seen as people, not target markets. We want to know we have been heard and feel a connection through the messaging to the people behind it. Businesses today have to put the humanity back into marketing. Or, they very well may fall by the wayside, replaced by someone we feel synergy with because, by golly, they get us!

Listening tools

There are a slew of social media listening tools out there. These are enhanced search engines, and they look for keywords, phrases or links to your website and report back to you what people are saying. Some tools are better than others. But, rather than dig into that here, I'll refer you to the resources section of the website for some favorite listening tools.

---

[11] There is No B2B or B2C: It's Human to Human http://j.mp/1NXQIiR

Listen for opportunity

Depending on your business model, listening to social media can reap great rewards, even if you aren't using that specific social network for your business.

Let's say your competitor just released a new product line that will compete against yours. Listening to social networks for mention of their product can reveal both it's best characteristics and the problems users are encountering. This is invaluable data to inform your own development and marketing.

I'm not saying you should exploit their weaknesses in public and call them out on the carpet. That behavior rarely ends well on the internet (or anywhere). Rather, use what you hear to improve your product or create a storyline about the qualities of your product that solve the problems better.

Social listening tools are a gold mine for journalists

In an April 2015 meeting of the Senate Finance Committee, Pat Roberts, the senior Senator from Kansas, took the floor to ask a question. Unfortunately for Roberts, he'd neglected to turn off his cellphone and his phone broadcast his ringtone, the hit song from the animated film Frozen, "Let It Go". The room went still and all turned to Roberts, who had the presence of mind to say, simply, "*Just let it go, mister*".

That's when the team at NowThis [12] leapt into action. Recognizing an eminently shareable event, they located the video of the incident and posted on social networks. In minutes, they saw hundreds of mentions. CNN picked it up and ran with it a few minutes later. Roberts' social media team responded with a tweet, "Somebody had to tell the Obama Administration to "Let it

---

[12] NowThis http://nowthisnews.com/

go." #forthegrandkids." [13] A few hundred replies and retweets immediately popped up, most of them negative. There were Vine clips made of it and shared by other users. Facebook lit up with the story. Roberts did not respond to the comments, the internet moved on and forgot about it.

What's the lesson here? The team at NowThis was on the ball and ready to respond to a tweet that tipped them off in just moments. They were using a social listening tool called Dataminr, which filters through the millions of social posts looking for interesting data based on search criteria they've set up. You can use this and other similar tools just as easily to find out what people are talking about in real time and join in those conversations yourself.

I'm not suggesting you jump on the bandwagon of negative news stories and shaming that is the ugly underbelly of the internet. Remember, you are who and what you associate with and everything will be taken out of context at some point. If you dive into negativity, that negative post will surface somewhere totally out of context in the future and it could be nasty. Above all, BE NICE.

What these tools do is allow you to isolate sentiment and useful information you can use to learn more about your market and what they want. They can also help you see what topics are popular online, enabling you to be involved in those conversations.

Another social listening tool, CrowdTangle.com, is thought to be the secret sauce behind Upworthy's success. Using this tool, you can see what the crowd is thinking about and then be more aware and responsive with your social media posting schedule. That is, if

---

[13] Pat Robert's tweet http://j.mp/patfrozen

you can respond quickly. Trends come and go in a heartbeat, and catching them may well be an elusive task.

Instead of trying to be ahead of the news curve every day, think about what you can do to engage users interested in the same things you are.

Remember that list in Chapter 4 of things to talk about for Two Dog Leash? Setting them up in a listening tool will bring you piles and piles of information to sift through and share with your networks. That's what curation is. Finding and sharing the information, always with credit to the source, that adds value and interest to your network.

Unless you are a journalist or have a large staff, this data sifting can be truly overwhelming. The data is enticing, to be sure. But, as CMOs sign up for the latest and greatest social media listening tools, sold to them by dangling shiny accessible data in front of their eyes in a flashy webinar, few know what to do with the data they are gathering.

Gathering big data is relatively easy. Run a few algorithms and the magic happens, right? But big data is simply too deep for most of us to filter and use on a day-to-day basis. The big data has to be converted to the smaller bite-sized chunks that are really useful to us. This is where careful planning and setup of your listening tools is crucial.

Use cases for social listening

For the typical business, there are some basic strategies to use listening data in a more manageable way. Sure, you won't get everything, but you'll get enough. Here are a few to consider and see if they are a good fit for your business.

Target campaigns and content

When you are releasing a new e-book or slide presentation, see what other information is out there, created by others, that you can share to support your theories. Even if the content they created was published a while ago, if it is still current, share it. The author will thank you and may even share or comment on your work. Anyone making a buying decision will appreciate the additional information and look to you as a resource for more of the same.

One oddity of social networking is that people see two names together and then carry that association forward in their heads. They're not sure why they think you go together, but they know you do. This can be advantageous when supporting partners or potential partners by simply sharing quality information.

Trending news

Searching trending topics for news to share with your networks, your team, and your users can support your day-to-day messaging. Again, you want to be a resource within your community of practice. Add value and they'll remember you.

Social rules

Set up social listening rules to find content, then add your own take on it to make it even more valuable to your network. Create thoughtful posts that people relate to in real time and share with their friends. If you're posting an article to LinkedIn, for example, don't just post the link. Give your opinion or share insights on the article. Add value.

Support traditional marketing

Rather than filtering through the fire hose of big data, drill down to small points that will accent your existing traditional marketing, ad buys, or your newsletter. If you are running a TV spot, carry that messaging into your social accounts as well. Ask people if they saw it and what they thought. Share the b-roll or out-takes on social. Tell the story and share links for pertinent information.

Wrap-up posts

If you've got a newsletter or a blog, turn the content you've curated through listening into a weekly wrap-up blog post or newsletter. Those of us who don't have time to sift through that data ourselves appreciate the effort!

****

Do This

Set up your social listening tools, as well as a schedule for when you are going to use them. These things can drift off the radar if it's not on your calendar. Make a point of sharing what you find with the appropriate teams in sales, marketing, and customer service, too.

Mindful Moment

Listening is great, but *hearing* is even better! Do you understand what people are saying, or do you just automatically respond? Take a second to process before responding or sharing. Read the whole post, not just the title. If someone asks a question, ask a question to clarify before you answer, if need be. Listen first and then be responsive instead of reactive.

CHAPTER SIX

Finding the Content

"What really decides consumers to buy or not to buy is the content of your advertising, not its form."
- David Ogilvy

Wouldn't it be great if we had unlimited potential to tell our story and spin it in such a way that everyone wanted our product? Make it ready for every known platform and medium? Have our market so excited to read it that they line up waiting for our e-books and whitepapers?

Sure, it would! But that's not very realistic. So, how do we create all this content to attract people to us without being spammy and repackaging press releases and whitepapers? Where do we start?

Start with your intentions
Your intentions should always be the focus of your social marketing strategy.
- What are your goals and how will you measure success?
- What is your value proposition to the customer?

- Who do you want to engage?
- What actions do you want them to take?
- What do you want to teach them?

Once you are clear on your intentions, they inform your narrative, the story that grabs the reader and draws them to you. Your narrative should wind itself through every single piece of marketing you create because it's your mission, your storyline, the thing that makes you different from everyone else.

Think about what that narrative is and write it down. Put it on the wall. Put it on your computer. Put it everywhere in the office, so that people know what you stand for and what you're all about. It may need some fine-tuning from time to time, and that's OK, this is the plot of ground you stand on. Where you take it from there is up to you and the whims of your customer base.

Once you've defined the narrative, you can start to look for content related to it.

Remember - you can't continue to flood consumers with messaging to buy, buy, buy without providing a compelling story and offering them something of value to engage with you.

In "Youtility: Why Smart Marketing Is about Help Not Hype"[14], Jay Baer writes: *"Today's consumers are staring at an invitation avalanche, with every company asking for likes, follows, clicks and attention. This is on top of all the legacy advertising that envelops us like a straitjacket. There are only two ways for companies to*

---

[14] Youtility: Why Smart Marketing Is about Help Not Hype
http://j.mp/1NXStwC

break through in an environment that is unprecedented in its competitiveness and cacophony. They can be "amazing" or they can be useful."

Being consistently amazing is tough. But, a few moments of brilliance supported by a lot of truly valuable content will win you a following that not only looks forward to hearing from you, but also buys from you because they trust you, maybe even *like* you. And they will tell their friends.

Let's get to work
In the last chapter, you defined your niche and who you want to talk to. Now you can use that information, along with your narrative, to create and source content that brings the two halves together.

Where do you find useful content?
You would not believe how many people think the only content that matters is the content they write. That's a very small-minded way to look at the world. Is your voice the only one that's important in a conversation? If you think so, you should just close this book right now because it isn't going to work for you.

Effective social marketing is about sharing, compassion, kindness, and, most especially, generosity. It's about being mindful, and that means by focusing on the entire world in a holistic sort of way. What do people care about that matters to you? What do people have to say that is aligned with the intention you have for marketing? Sharing generously gives kudos to the other smart people in your universe. Sharing their thoughts aligns your stars with theirs and makes the world a better, warmer place for both of you. Generosity is always returned, often in ways you could never have foreseen.

I don't care what market niche you are working in, there are people out there writing insightful blog posts and articles that your customer would love to know about. If it educates, entertains, or engages you and aligns in some way with your own story, then it is probably interesting to your market, too. Finding ways to share it, generally with a comment, is a fantastic source of useful material to share and discuss with your networks. We call this "curating."

Curate, according to Google:
Curate (verb) cu·rate \ˈkyu̇r-ˌāt, kyu̇-ˈrāt\
-to select, organize, and look after the items in (a collection or exhibition)
-to select, organize, and present (online content, merchandise, information, etc.), typically using professional or expert knowledge

For social media marketing purposes, curation of content is gathering relevant information to share with your networks for the purpose of education or discussion, or to support your position around specific topics and areas of expertise.

Simply put, you don't have to reinvent the wheel with brand new content every single post. You can curate content. You can retweet. You can do searches to find things that tie in with what your mission, your narrative, your values, and your story. Find videos on popular networks and embed them in a blog post with your commentary.

Mind you, that doesn't mean you can take other people's content and call it your own, sharing it willy-nilly across the universe. That's called plagiarism, and it is most definitely NOT OK. Share relevant content freely, but always credit the source. Check the resources section of the website for guidelines on content curation and some wonderful tools to make it easy as pie.

Social generosity

If you really want to be recognized as a thought leader in your industry in order to promote yourself or your business, generosity is going to be a key element in your strategy. Sharing news and information related to what you customers, cohorts, and even competitors need to know creates a trust relationship that you cannot buy. When people know you are consistently on top of the news and that you share information without worrying about getting credit for it, you are earning the trust of your readers, as well as the gratitude and trust of the original author.

Reciprocity

When you share my content, I am quite likely to thank you. I may thank you with a message, an email, or even a phone call. You are now top of mind for me. I may even remember that we haven't met face-to-face for a while and invite you out to lunch. If you share a blog post on Twitter, I will probably thank you and then go look at your profile to see if I can return the favor and share something of yours or add a comment to deepen a conversation.

Share great quotes, always with credit

Another one of the oddities about social media is that people ascribe a statement, post or tweet to the first person whose post they see it in. If you share something Seth Godin or Bill Ford, the CEO of Ford Motor Company, said, your followers will associate you with the quote and also think of you as connected to the person quoted. They assume great minds think alike.

This isn't intended to mislead. But, if it inspires you, it may well inspire others in your industry. Sharing great, useful information with your networks results in them looking to you as an important figure in their circle of connections.

Maybe you're a Ford dealership. You share Ford's stories because they are relevant to you and your market, being mindful of their interests in the qualities of the car, as well as issues that come up like recalls or choosing the right car for them, even if it's not a Ford. In the eyes of your followers you represent Ford Motor Company. You now have a responsibility to your followers to give them current, accurate, and useful information about the auto industry. When they look to you for this information and rely on you as a source, they are more likely to look kindly on the occasional sales pitch or even a social ad or two, because they trust you.

Curating content from news articles, for example, is a great way to share information with your network and expand their idea of who you are. Depending on your personal brand, you may want to avoid hot button topics but stick to the things that interest you. Create a relationship and a persona that people can relate to and want to know better.

What you're trying to build here is what we call a community of practice. A community of practice is a group of people who have similar interests and share information amongst themselves to the betterment of all. These similar interests bind us together, whether we are competitors, amateurs, or people just interested in the same thing.

We all want to talk about these particular issues, and so members of the community of practice support each other by sharing information. This is a wonderful thing for a sales team. For example, create an account on Twitter or Google+ or a Facebook group which allows you to share information among the team. As news comes up, somebody on the team shares that data on a regular basis in order to keep things flowing smoothly. Someone also decides what of that information can be curated into your social media accounts. Everyone has something to say about it, they share with their cohort in their own words and you're all very well informed. So is your network.

Social media, by the way, is a wonderful tool for professional development, and that's something a community of practice speaks to. Even if they are technically competitors, sharing news relevant to both companies is still a good idea, and a way to take a mindful approach to how you work.

On being first

Who doesn't want to be the first one to tell everyone else the latest news or find the latest tool to end all tools? Yeah, these days that can be a challenge, at least in my industry. When a start-up launches, the tech news is all over it and there is always a flurry of discussion. I expect it's the same in your industry, too. So, if you can't be first with the news, what should you do?

Share other people's posts about whatever the shiny new thing is, but add your own voice to the discussion. Take a different perspective. Tell us how it applies to us and how it applies to you. Provide that added value to your readers and they will be grateful to not have to go dig through material to learn it themselves.

If you do have special access or insight, being first can be a huge boon to your visibility. In this video clip with Jason Falls, [15]he talks

---

[15] The Friday Hangout with Jason Falls https://youtu.be/LVSQRRoPS10

about how his special insight into a story turned into media hits, a guest spot on the BBC, and much more. It was his unique viewpoint and willingness to evaluate the situation that made him stand out. With a thoughtful reaction to the news of the day, instead of the same thing everyone else was sharing, he added value that was noticed.

Talk to your team

Find out who the natural mavens are in your organization. (Maven is a Yiddish word for someone who accumulates knowledge. Generally, mavens yearn to share their knowledge and are a valuable company resource). There always is a maven, you know. Very often, it's someone who isn't completely obvious, but everybody goes to them with their questions. Ask these mavens who they respect and listen to online and start connecting, or at least following them for those nuggets of wisdom previously outside your field of view.

Engineers, for example, can be incredibly passionate about what they've done, what they've created, and the problem that this product solves. They have tons of information to share with the world, but sometimes they are in the background, not in the forefront. They're probably not the focus of a lot of marketing campaigns, even though they may be the smartest people in the room. But, they can be. Go find your engineer. Ask her what the challenges were about solving this problem. Ask her what the challenges were she ran into as she developed it. Ask what she learned along the way, both about the problem and about the solution. Now write it up and share it.

You don't have to give away all your deep corporate secrets and your archive of proprietary information here, but you can share the passion that engineer has for what they do and the problem they solve. If you do that, it will go a long way in convincing your customers how important and valuable your product is and showing the amount of love that went into creating it to solve their problem.

Ask your engineers who they listen to on social networks and where they have conversations of value. These may be places you can find an audience for your brand.

"Invite ALL Your Internal Stakeholders into Your Social Strategy. It's EVERYONE'S Social Media Now!" - Neal Schaffer

Marketing and PR

The marketing and PR team need to be on board here. It can be a difficult battle. Don't try to get around it. Make time to talk to everyone in your group about your goals. Find out what their frustrations and questions are, and pool your ideas for marketing the company in a mindful way. Is there resistance? Why? What do you need to do in order to help them understand the value in your direction and how it will make their job easier?

Do some searches with those listening tools to show them examples of the type of marketing you want to do and how it is successful. Use some of the examples in the chapter on marketing fails to demonstrate how marketing thoughtlessly on social media can go wrong as a lesson on what to avoid.

The gatekeeper

When you go into an office, the first person you see is the receptionist. She's the gatekeeper. It's her job to make sure that you don't talk to the CEO or anyone else behind the desk, unless you've got an appointment. She is there to safeguard the intellectual property and time of the company. She does a lot of things to put a wall up and protect the CEO. Think of Donna Paulsen in Suits or Joan Holloway in Mad Men as fabulous examples of a gatekeeper.

If you are the CEO, you should be talking to the gatekeeper and finding out:
- What kinds of questions do people ask her when they come in?
- What does she know about the company and how it works?
- Who is always talking about how much they love the company and products?
- What problems come up over and over?
- When those problems come up, who do they go to to solve them?

The gatekeeper has a unique viewpoint of how your office runs and how your product is perceived in the world. She's there when someone comes to meet a salesperson; she talks to people because that's what good mavens do. She mines information in case she needs it later and she does it in a human and personal way. She makes people comfortable and that makes it easy for them to learn, as well as become a resource for everyone. She has a unique perspective and one you should pay attention to and give great value to. Sit down regularly to touch base and, for god's sake, take her to lunch once in a while to really understand. LISTEN.

The sales team

Take the sales team to lunch, too. One at a time, so you can hear each one and respect their unique perspective. The sales team has a very different approach than the marketing team. The marketing team promotes what could be. The sales team is more about what is. Often, the two conflict, don't they? That's why it's very important you take the time to go and interview the sales team to find out what problems they're encountering in the field.

The sales team may know about a new product you should be developing, but be afraid to tell anybody because they don't want to get shot down. Find out what they know and then highlight them. Give them the wherewithal to help you understand what your customer wants. That's what social sales is all about! See the resources section for two excellent videos with Jill Rowley, the queen of the social sales movement, to understand more about this.

When you talk to your entire team, certain people will pop out. They're passionate about your business. They're passionate about the problem that you solve. They're passionate about the subject. When you can ignite those people and empower them to be a voice for the company, in any shape or form, you are really creating a way to connect with your customer base and your niche, and stand head and shoulders above your competitors.

I'm not saying that you should give them a microphone and let them run with it. I know it's very scary for a lot of businesses to empower their employees too much. Don't be afraid. These people are there because they want to be there. Find ways to make it work.

We often go into a company and find an engineer, a CEO, a salesperson, or a line worker who's passionate about the business and what the business does, the company's products, and the problems they solve. But they either aren't interested or don't have the time to participate on social. We'll sit down in a room and interview them. It'll be a very long interview.

We just let them talk and focus on listening, asking questions to extend the conversation without actually leading it. The point is to let them ramble, listen carefully, and record it. Not to catch them out on something, but to get them to relax so they let their passion show and share their knowledge.

If you do this mindfully, you'll find some nuggets of information in there you can share, and that you would probably miss if you were thinking about what you were going to say next. Instead, stay present and listen.

You might do interviews on video and cut the recording into several clips to share or a montage of nuggets of information. But, don't make them talking head videos. Those are so, so, so boring. Make them interesting. "Here's Alison, and she wanted to tell us why this chip is better than any chip you've ever seen before." Use images, slides or video clips to accentuate points and keep it visually interesting too.

Give people a voice that works for them
Maybe video isn't their thing. Maybe you take the audio, and send it out to be transcribed into text. Once it's transcribed, it can be used as a blog post, or to build an explainer video or infographic. It can be used to create any number of quote graphics. Maybe it's part of a white paper. Think about all the things you can do with that information. Drip it out over a period of time in your marketing material. Mix it in with curated content. Even if it's something that you don't want to share verbatim, it can spark an idea for someone else to write a story about.

One of the things about social media that makes it so amazing and so wonderful is that it's an opportunity for developing thought leadership.

"Leaders don't just lead; they create more leaders." -Tom Peters

Great leaders empower the people that they work with. If you empower your employees and find ways to enable them to create thought leadership, you are really, truly being a mindful business. Everyone benefits.

Enabling employee advocacy

In an interview on employee advocacy[16], Frank Strong, a PR expert, said that employees are the secret sauce to content marketing.

He puts processes in place to help employees understand how to share their knowledge and distribute content, but he doesn't want to over-restrict with rigid rules. Instead, he gives the employees left and right limits and then lets them run with it.

If a company can't trust their employees, who else can it trust? Yes, you need to have training, you need to make sure people aren't out there doing silly things, and they will, but you need to have trust in your employees...

Bottom line, your employees truly are a great content source. If you are not enabling them to share and celebrating their value, you are missing an opportunity.

Content from your clients

Talk to your clients. Find out what kind of things they like or don't like about your product or your competitors' products. Consider doing some form of testimonial or finding out what other things really interest them. If you include your clients in your community

---

[16] Frank Strong Video https://youtu.be/DvFzF1TiD7w

of practice and share information through social media, it can be amazingly powerful. So powerful that it is becoming the industry standard.

Just think about it. If you develop a following of your client base on a social media network and they start to look to you as a resource for information about anything in the industry, not just your product, suddenly you become invaluable to them. Even when they don't need your product, they'll still come and listen because you're sharing valuable information that helps them in their own jobs or lives.

One of the best cases for sharing without selling goes back over 100 years to John Deere's "The Furrow" magazine, first published in 1895.

The Furrow is not a sales tool; it's a magazine dedicated to the farmers, loaded with information they can put to use in their work. Initially, it may have been a bit advertorial, but then it grew and became more focused on crop rotations and other farming methods. Today it reaches over 2 million readers globally and, in addition to sharing techniques and visuals of farm life, also helps farmers manage their businesses more efficiently with the latest innovations.

Yes, there are sales opportunities included. But, it's clearly not the main focus of the content. It's about farming, farmers, and family. Of course, they also have a presence on several social media networks - with over 2 million fans on Facebook alone. This is a company that truly understands the power of generously sharing information with their community of practice. It's interesting to note that back copies of the Furrow have been known to sell on

Ebay for over $300. Clearly, collectors see the value in real content too.

Content from existing material
We all have content lurking around in the dusty recesses of our offices, or even our inboxes.

Start by pulling together all of the print and digital resources you have. Put them in a pile, grab some coffee, and read it all. Highlight what you can use. Pull out the concepts and topics you can build on in some way. Maybe it's just a quote or a link to relevant information. Maybe it's the foundation for a series of videos or blog posts.

Create and maintain a digital archive of all this usable information, so you can come back to it for ideas. Then, tailor a game plan for sharing this content, along with the content you are curating from other sources. Wind it around your narrative. Make this treasure trove of knowledge available to the social media team to chunk up into digestible pieces of information to share with your network.

I could go on and on here about the value of quality content and how to create it, but I'll leave that to the content experts. I highly suggest you get a copy of some of Joe Pulizzi's books, especially the now classic "Epic Content Marketing"[17].

Also, subscribe to the Content Marketing Institute[18] and some of the other resources on content marketing listed on the website. I

---

[17] Epic Content Marketing http://j.mp/1NXUk4q

[18] Content Marketing Institute http://j.mp/1NXUmJH

cannot stress enough the importance of quality content, whether you create it yourself or simply share it with your community.

Graphically speaking

A picture tells a thousand words? Yeah, and on social media sites a picture will grab your viewers. In 2015, Instagram grew 50% and passed 300 million users. Facebook claims the number of videos shared on their site topped 12 billion, almost a billion more than YouTube. Social media scientist Dan Zarella reviewed over 400,000 Tweets and reported [19] that those uploaded to Twitter with a picture had 94% more chances of being retweeted. Research at 3M Corporation concluded that we process a visual 60,000 times faster than text.

In his book, "Social Poetry[20]", Joel Comm filled each page with images he has shared on social networks. The images tell a story with a simple phrase and an eye-catching photo. Working your name, hashtag or username into an image can be a great marketing tool. When those images are shared by others, it demonstrates their trust in you. And now we trust you too, by association. Joel posts his images and they get shared across many networks, maybe even networks he's not using personally. What do you have to say?

Image creation tools

There is a list of image creation tools in the resources section, but Canva[21], co-created by Guy Kawasaki, is my personal favorite. You

---

[19] http://danzarrella.com/use-images-on-twitter-to-get-more-retweets.html

[20] http://www.amazon.com/Social-Poetry-Conversation-Inspirational-Entertaining/dp/1505617049

[21] Canva http://canva.com

can quickly create images for social media headers, avatars, blog posts or even slide share presentations - all without having a degree in graphic design, or even knowledge of Photoshop.

****

Do this

Set intentions for how you're going to use your content. How many pieces of social content can you get from one source - like a blog post or news piece? How many times can you re-share that content with your community of practice over a period? More information about this can be found in the resources section, as well as some tools to build out content calendars and things that will really help you get going with sharing your social media and seeing how you can really take one piece of content and make multiple pieces of content out of it.

Mindful Moment

We are often surprised by how much we and our team know and can share with the world. When we create content with an eye toward our intention for our relationship with the viewer, we are more efficient and effective in reaching our market.

CHAPTER SEVEN

Influencer outreach

"The web isn't really made up of algorithms. It's made of people. In all their frustrating, imperfect, and complicated glory."
- Sonia Simone

Influencer outreach has become a hot topic of late for businesses wanting to see more buzz about their brand on social media sites. Social media influence is measured by the number of people an individual influencer can encourage to take an action. This might be signing a petition, donating to a cause or buying a product. Every niche has it's own set of influencers and, in many cases, it's own set of rules.

Some influencers focus on sharing product information through reviews or paid posts and endorsements. Others have more of a journalistic bent and are not paid, just passionate about the topic and willing to support aligning brands or causes.

Lots of people will tell you that Social Media Influencers are the key to social media marketing. But, how do we decide who has influence? Is influence based on number of connections? Klout, Peer Index or Kred score? A combination of all of the above? How do you identify influencers? And what do you do with that information, once you think you know who they are?

The short answer is all, and none, of the above. There is no cookie cutter answer. Every business is different and there are many permutations of what makes up an influencer. You have to fine-tune the list of influencers to suit your goals for reaching out to them in the first place.

People who have real influence have the respect of their following. The people who connect with them look to them for thought leadership and insight. At the same time, they know that the influencer respects and reveres those who follow them. They feel appreciated and so they also develop trust for the influencer and their opinions.

Locating and qualifying an influencer is an arduous task. On the website, I've posted a link to my "14 Step Guide to Influencer Outreach" in the resources section.

There are a dozen "influencer networks" that can help you find candidates. There are also tools like BuzzSumo, BuzzStream, GetLittleBird, and Mention's Influencer score to help you get started. But, in the end, you still have to filter them to find the right people for you. Here's an idea of how it works:

- Start by being very clear of your intentions for this campaign, what you want from influencers, and what you can offer them.

- Locate people who have true influence as opposed to a fake follower count.

- Find people others listen to and are inspired to take action by.

- Determine whether or not you expect them to write a blog post or article about your product, and if they are qualified to do so.

- See if they have an established influence on your topic with their users.

- Check their communication style to see if it is a good fit with your brand.

- Always nurture a relationship before you ask them for anything. What can you do for them? Will you share their blog posts? Answer or ask a question?

- Decide what the best communication method is for each blogger.

- Know what you want them to do and how you will track their success.

- Craft an email or reach out through social media to gauge their interest. Be considerate of they way they communicate and never send a bulk inquiry email. Be personable and professional.

That's a lot of work for each and every influencer, isn't it? Yes, it is. But, it's essential to finding real influencers, as opposed to those people who practice black hat SEO, buy followers on social media networks to get inflated fan counts, or participate in other practices that make them appear to have influence, when in reality it's all buzz and no substance. Real relationships are hard work!

You're in this for the long-game. An influencer who has a good relationship with you is likely to continue to support you down the road, whether as part of a campaign or not. You will share information useful to them and their network, as well as sharing their posts when they are relevant to your own network.

Once you develop a reciprocal relationship with an influencer, you are in a much better position to talk to them about sharing your story. You can help them to understand what message you need to get out and they're willing to help you because they know you've been generous and helped them in the past.

Paying influencers is common and there are plenty of reasons to pay an influencer for their time, but be careful with this. There are many so-called influencers out there who have huge followings but when you really dig into their profiles and analyze them, you may find they don't get a lot of action on what they post. If nobody cares about what they share, then how are they valuable for you? Make sure they are truly influencing and interacting with the market you want to reach before you put a lot of time or energy into that particular influencer.

If you do decided to pay an influencer with free products or cold hard cash, be sure that you are in compliance with the FTC's regulations. It's important to disclose any paid relationship as it is, essentially, an ad.

******

Do This

Take some time to identify people in your social networks who have true influence with their own networks. Get to know them and look for ways to support them. Give them a little love! Talk to them.

Mindful Moment

You can have influence on one or several topics by carefully cultivating information and sharing it with people who are interested in that area. Staying focused helps people have a clear picture of who you are and what you represent. They can then start looking to you for thought leadership on that topic.

CHAPTER EIGHT

Social Customer Service

"Your most unhappy customers are your greatest source of learning." - Bill Gates

Do I need to explain why social media is crucial to customer service, both on and off line? Well, just in case, here it is: consumers expect businesses to be present on social networks. Beyond using social media for marketing, you've got to be ready to resolve customer issues, as well. A great customer service experience is most certainly a boon to marketing.

When customers post a question, a problem or simply want to tell you how great you are, you don't want to disappoint them. Be on social and they will find you. If you're not on social, they will tell all their friends how it sucks that you're not on social. And that sucks for you.

"Your customers don't care about you. They don't care about your product or service. They care about themselves, their dreams, their goals." -Steve Jobs

J.D. Power and Associates' recent Social Media Benchmark[22] study found that 67% of consumers have used a company's social media page for service. It also found that 43% of consumers aged 18-29 are more likely to use brands' social media sites for service interactions than any other method of communication.

Brands like Wells Fargo, Bank of America, Media Temple, Hyatt Hotels, JetBlue, Southwest Airlines, American Airlines, and US Airways are all monitoring the social media airwaves for indications of customer dissatisfaction. It's become commonplace for a traveler stuck in an airport to Tweet the airline for alternative flight information and even rebooking.

Some brands keep a separate channel just for customer service. For example, Hyatt hotels offers accounts for some of the properties, a news channel (@HyattTweets), and a concierge twitter (@HyattConcierge). Their message? *"In a Hyatt world, service extends beyond the walls of our hotel"*.

The concierge account scours Twitter for questions, complaints, and kudos. Then they answer the questions, reach out to unhappy travelers with a kind word, congratulate people on their photos, and, in general, keep a positive, helpful vibe going. Bravo!

On Facebook, each hotel handles customer service on their own page, most likely because search works differently on Facebook.

---

[22] http://www.jdpower.com/press-releases/2013-social-media-benchmark-study

The social team will look for mentions of the hotel, but when people write posts visible only to their friends the Hyatt team can't find it because of Facebook's privacy settings. Every network needs a different approach.

A customer service channel should be full of problem-solving and thank you's to your customers, not marketing. That said, this is clearly marketing in a different form.

Everyone wants to be heard and served, right? If we see you serving your customer with kindness and compassion, those warm and fuzzy feelings will linger and we will remember you when we have to make a buying decision.

Not everyone can dedicate a team to it, but if you can, it can be a powerful tool for your customers and for developing brand recognition. It rarely makes sense to have the whole conversation online. Personal details and dirty laundry don't have to clog up the network. Many brands will simply take the interaction off-line after first contact and solve it through direct messages, SMS, on the phone, or even in person.

If you are serving your customers through social channels, remember to let the customer know that. Put it on your website, in your emails and on your promotional material. Let them know, too, that there is a human on the other end of the social account by using initials at the end of each post. (For example, I use >JF at the end of my posts when acting for a client). This lets customers identify with that person and feel more personally connected to your company. If you can't be online 24/7, let people know when you are available and give them another avenue to reach service when you are not. This could be a phone number or other contact information.

Zappos does this beautifully. As one customer service rep leaves, they sign off: *"Goodnight folks, Tami is out for the evening. Have a good one!"* or some such thing. When they come online, they let people know in a cheery way. *"Hey, it's Sam, here to answer questions for you. How's your day going?"*

This personalization sets people at ease and at the same time lets people know you're ready to serve.

You've got search

Customer service online is part sleuthing, too. Not all of the customers will be able or care to find you. Search tools discussed in the chapter on listening can go a long way toward finding someone who is mildly unhappy or having an issue before they become a problem. Use these tools and respond in a friendly and helpful manner.

What about the haters?

Oh, this is such a common question, and I have a very simple answer. Taking a helpful and compassionate approach can turn haters into evangelists. It's all about your attitude.

Sure, there may be unhappy people out there bad-mouthing your company. If you aren't at least listening on social networks for this feedback, you're missing the boat. If you respond and talk to the customer, you can reap many rewards.

Discover a flaw with your product before it becomes a bigger issue.

Have an opportunity to improve your product or create a new product altogether.

See a problem with your competitor's product in a new light and how you can do it better.

Turn a brand hater into a brand evangelist.

Show the world you respect your customer.

Honestly, most of the time, people just want to be heard. Today they expect to be heard through social channels.

Start with thank you
Thank the disgruntled customer for bringing their issue to your attention and then listen to whatever problems they are having. Do whatever it takes to resolve it in a timely and realistic manner. A newly happy customer on social networks can become an evangelist for your brand.

Apologize
Don't give a namby-pamby toothless apology. Put some heartfelt compassion into it. Acknowledge the issue and promise to follow up offline if necessary. Then DO it.

Respond, not react
We often have a knee-jerk reaction to a negative response online. We get defensive about the product we love. Sometimes we fight back or justify taking action without full knowledge. There is no way that is going to come out well. Pause. Listen, consider, and ask questions. Take a breath before you respond.

An authentic and mindful response beats a knee-jerk reaction every single time.

Think service
If a customer service agent is well trained, they already know how to deal with an angry customer. Breath, listen, breath again, respond with compassion and kindness. Don't let their anger transfer to you. This is the way a mindful social marketer responds on a social network, too. A social marketer has a huge advantage. They have time to react. They're not on the phone or dealing with

the customer face-to-face. They have time to pause, consider, and carefully respond, instead of reacting. Take a walk if you have to. Always breathe.

If you want social engagement and seek to truly serve, expect people to talk to you and think about how you're going to talk back to them.

- Be curious.

- Ask questions and give a damn about the answers.

- Pay attention to the answers you give to questions and expand on them, add a link to more information just to help people.

- Continue the conversation you've started by being interested in the person on the other side.

- Be someone we want to know and feel connected with because you're worth our time, and we feel valued.

- Always close a customer service interaction with a kind word.

****

Do This

Take the elements of mindfulness from the first chapter and think about how you can be more present and curious about your customer and your business category. Make a list of common questions and answers, then write them in a human, compassionate voice so they don't feel so canned. Enable the team to customize these as needed to fit their individual personalities and each customer, instead of posting from a script.

Mindful Moment

Empowering our staff helps get the message out more clearly and to a broader audience via real one-on-one communication. Beyond that, it instills a feeling in your team that you trust them with the ball. This impacts your entire workforce even if they don't participate on social networks. Doesn't everyone feel better working somewhere they are trusted, empowered, and happy?

CHAPTER NINE

Social Sales

"My readers and my audiences have turned into my followers. They are more than interested in what I have to say in the subjects of sales, loyalty, attitude, networking, business social media, and becoming a trusted advisor." - Jeffrey Gitomer

Anyone who talks about social media and business eventually asks or answers the big question about social media marketing, "What's the ROI?" While this book is certainly not about social sales in itself, marketing has a big role in creating opportunities for sales.

I recently had a video interview with social sales advocate Jill Rowley. Here's a brief excerpt of that conversation.[23]

Janet: What kind of metrics would a salesperson be using?

---

[23] Jill Rowley interview https://youtu.be/uPWRUgDObzl

Obviously, sales is one of those metrics, but it's only one of them. What else can we be looking at to see if you're successful at social selling?

Jill: At the end of the day, the rubber meets the road with revenue. At the end of the day, that is the true measure of whether social selling has an impact on your performance as a sales rep. Until we stop measuring salespeople on revenue, which that's probably not going to happen. Although I do think I'd like to see reps being compensated not just for closing the deal, but for customer advocacy. If that customer ultimately turns into a reference, to an advocate who influences other buyers to buy, the rep . . . there should be a portion of compensation tied to the customer being happy.

This is futuristic. I know sales leaders all over the world aren't ready for this. Sales reps all over the world aren't ready for this. But when customers are buying more today based on the experience and the value generated, we have to move in that direction.

Directionally, what are some metrics to measure to see if the rep is showing behaviors and activities that contribute to social selling? I would say they are kind of the vanity metrics, right? They are the size of the network. On LinkedIn, it's the number of connections you have. But it isn't just the quantity of connections, it's the quality of the network.

Janet: What about tracking, as they move the traditional funnel? If you look at their first entry into social media conversations, maybe they're just filling the top of that funnel. But as it goes down, how can they track those and what are they looking for? I will never agree that sheer volume of numbers is going to be a metric to judge anything. They have to be engaged. They have to be useful to you or they really are just that top of the funnel and you're kind of praying that something good is going to happen someday.

Jill: I like to be very specific about what a social seller does. Today, I had a call at noon Pacific. The meeting invite included the names of the people who would be in the meeting. As a good social seller, I Googled every single person who was going to be in the meeting. One of the women has four sons and is a green belt in Taekwondo. One of the women has a recommendation on her LinkedIn profile talking about how she is so organized, so focused. Her ability to get shit done is incredible. Then another woman had some personal interests. She's into photography.

That's social selling. That's doing that research. Now, I could take it a step further. We're negotiating the contract. How about I send an article to Janet about moms who do Taekwondo? Relevant to build a relationship that drives revenue. We've never had more access to personal information about people and we can leverage that, again, build better relationships with potential buyers.

Janet: Right. Those are the same kind of tools really good salespeople, through the ages, have always known. When I was a restaurant chef, they knew what little snacks to bring me. They knew what I wanted for Christmas. The salespeople would come in and they had a dossier on every single person that they did business with. Now social allows us to go a lot deeper with that. I think that's something that the real salespeople, the ones who really get how to sell and build relationships see that in social.

Jill: Social selling is one small sliver of the overall sales enablement, sales effectiveness, sales performance, sales productivity puzzle. I am not the evangelist saying "Social selling is the only thing you need to invest in and if you invest in social selling, your numbers will be made." That's not what I'm trying to tell anybody.

When I have a conversation about social selling, a lot of times I'm only talking about social selling, but this is in a much broader conversation. There's tons of bad sales reps all over the world.

There are tons of under-performing sales reps all over the world. With more information and more technology and more tools and more process and more methodology and more metrics, we're not getting better.

The overall numbers aren't getting significantly better when we have more awareness, more technology, more tools. It's not getting better.

Janet: Is that a trading issue? Or is it an intrinsic knowledge? Are you a natural salesperson or not?

Jill: I think attitude, behavior, technique and I'll quote Sandler. I just actually had a quick call with their CEO. Sandler Training is one option to train your sales team. Buying has changed more in the past 10 years than it has in the past 100. The way that people buy has changed dramatically.

Janet: Because we're better informed or?

Jill: Yeah. We can self-educate. We don't actually have to engage with sales until much later in our buying process. We don't want to. I don't answer the phone.

Janet: We go direct, right? Depending on the purchase.

Jill: Even in B2B, right? We either go to the Internet or we go to our network. I spoke with a woman yesterday, she bought Eloqua from me at two different companies. She's at a company that they're starting to invest in customer marketing. They spend all of their time and energy on customer acquisition. That sales team, it's hunters. They go out and they hunt new logos and they take down new deals. I know, the language in sales is so bad.
Janet: I'm always so amused by it.

Jill: It's so gross. "Prospecting. I'm going to go prospect." Ugh. "I'm going to go hunt and I'm going to farm my accounts." It's crazy. She reached out and they're trying to invest in customer marketing. My first comment to her was, "Customer marketing is old-school. Customer engagement is new school."

Janet: Can you define the difference between those two?

Jill: At someone, with someone.

Janet: Push versus pull.

Jill: Yep. "In it for me, gotta get more from you. I've got to up-sell, I've got to cross-sell." To, "How are we going to do this together? We're going to make each other better. We have a community of people like you who are doing interesting things and I'm going to connect you to that community and that ecosystem and that knowledge base and I'm going to impart best practices. Because of all of the giving that I'm doing for you and making you better, you're going to want to help make us better by referring us business, by sharing news and information and events and advocacy." We're a community, not marketing.

Janet: Yeah. With that in mind, when we talk to salespeople about doing social business or we talk to them about using social networks to prospect or any of the things that they're used to doing, the first thing you get is, "I don't have time for that. It's too much work. It's too hard. It's going to take all my time. I don't know how to start." How can we take that kind of mentality and sure, you can show them results, but they still aren't going to get it and they're going to try really, really hard for about a week and then they're going to go, "Okay, that doesn't work," and they're going to walk away. How do we help them to engage better and see results quickly enough that they actually stick with it?

101

Jill: Yeah, and that's a great question. What I see most often is a lot of random acts of social, social selling happening within organizations. There's a maturity curve. We're in the very beginning stages of understanding we need to do social selling, what the heck it is and how the heck to do it. There aren't many companies that are putting the necessary and appropriate attention to up-leveling the skills of their sales organization.

Done right, which requires an investment in people and in dollars, you would have a formal project owner. That project owner would realize, "I need to have cross-functional input and collaboration from marketing." Because marketing supplies the content. Marketing is best positioned to identify who are the influential smarty-pants people that influence your customers, your buyers, your prospects.

You need marketing. You need sales leadership. Because you need the leadership saying, "We're not going to smile and dial. We're going to reach and teach," right?

As I said, this book isn't about sales. There are great social sales experts like Jill who can give you much better advice than I about sales, but I will share my take on this.

Social media is rarely, if ever, a direct marketing channel. Yes, we can warm up a lead, or even bring a customer in the door to consider a purchase, but they still need to make the ultimate decision to buy.

Support direct marketing with social media. You might include a hashtag in a direct mail piece, a radio ad or a TV commercial. Be sure that all of your marketing has links to your social channels and be sure that information is readily seen in your brick and mortar store, if you have one.

Let's think for a moment about how great-really great-salespeople deal with initiating a sale.

Do they just walk up to someone at random on the street and say, "Hi, my name is Ginny and you've GOT to buy this product!" without ever knowing anything about the person, what they need, or warming up the prospect with some friendly remarks first? No, they never do that. Why not? Well, first, because it's just rude. Second, because it's stupid.

Any good salesperson gets to know their market first and how their product solves the market's pain points. They spend hours working on the language they'll use in different scenarios, as well as projecting the questions that may come up and how they will answer them. They plan based on the needs and wants of the buyers. They put themselves in the buyers' shoes.

In these days of instant information, good salespeople search Google and social networks to find out more about a prospect before they even call them. If they are smart social users, they will follow the person or brand on Twitter, join a group they're in on LinkedIn, follow the company, and engage in tangential conversations to become part of the person's social network before they connect. They'll set up listening tools to hear what the crowd has to say and what their needs are, too.

Good salespeople use what they learn online to make an intelligent approach. They'll nurture these relationships through the stages of awareness, recognition and friendship, creating an easy transition to talking about product, services and sales. Even if they don't use social media to connect with the person, they will call and make an appointment, have a short conversation about the prospects' needs, and maybe even buy lunch first, before they start asking for the sale.

Good sales relationships are nurtured, and the beauty of social media is the ability to nurture many more leads in one day than you possibly could face-to-face.

So, when I hear someone refer to social as a "sales channel" as though piping in a bunch of product mentions is going to instantly make you popular and better looking to a consumer, I cringe. Sales is now and will always be about relationships and hard work.

I love dealing with talented salespeople. Sometimes I'll buy from them simply because they are so good at their job, I just want to support them. I will choose a store or a vendor because of the caliber of sales. Think about it, salespeople have always been social. It's in their nature. They get to know you, what you like, how to please you and bring you back for more. That's their job and, with the good ones, it's their passion.

What are the traits of a good salesperson?
- Knowledge of the product and industry
- Understands competitors, as well as their products and markets
- Willing to listen to what the market wants and what their issues are
- Asks the right questions
- Keeps in touch with clients and prospects

Now let's look at how a salesperson works within a social business.

Knowledge of the product and industry

With social media listening tools[24], you can stay a step ahead of industry news, public perception of the industry, and of your own products. Following a few trade blogs can show where the industry is going and perhaps alternative uses for the product that may have slipped under the radar. You may also find opportunities to correct misconceptions and solve peoples' pain points. See a complaint about your product online as an opportunity to engage that user, solve their problem, and turn them into an advocate.

Understand competitors, as well as their products and markets

Using those same listening tools, find out what the competition is up to. Read customer feedback and look for opportunities to beat the competitor to the punch with new messaging online that highlights your own product-which just happens to have the feature that is missing in the competitors'. Become an industry resource and when people need a solution to a problem, who are they gonna go to?

Be willing to listen to what the market wants and what their issues are

This is different than knowing what you want to sell to the market. Listen long enough and you'll soon see patterns developing in what people talk about around the industry. They'll tell you what the flaws in the product are and how to fix it. They'll tell you if they use another product instead because it has just the

---

[24] http://janetfouts.com/listen/

add-ons they need to get the job done. They'll tell you when they are thinking about making a purchase.

Ask the right questions
Needless to say, you have to ask good questions, too, and then listen to the answers. Think of social media as a huge focus group. You can pose a single question on 20 different platforms, collate the answers and have a completely different perspective on what your customers need. Rinse, repeat.

Keep in touch with clients and prospects
Never has it been easier to keep in touch with clients. Social CRM tools like Salesforce, Hubspot and Nimble allow us to see what prospects and clients are saying on social media sites and create relationships with them before and beyond the sale. Paying attention to what they care about in the world gives you more opportunities to deepen relationships and create warm leads. Who doesn't love a nice warm sales lead?

****

Do this
Talk to your sales team about how they research leads now. See what the correlation is between what they're doing now and good social research. Give them training in social media listening tools so they can continue to learn and grow more qualified leads. Create a discussion channel to share information between marketing and sales.

Mindful moment
There is nothing surprising to a salesperson about social sales, but they may not have had the opportunity to see it for what it is. Many sales folks are trained to mine leads from databases or have

them delivered to them by their sales manager. What they do with those leads and how they nurture the relationships makes the difference between a good salesperson and a great one. When you enable them with social media tools and training you'll see the good ones light up like a roman candle.

CHAPTER TEN

When it all goes horribly wrong

"The proactive approach to a mistake is to acknowledge it instantly, correct and learn from it."
- Stephen Covey

No matter how mindful you are of what you write online, everyone makes mistakes. It's how you react to mistakes that can make the difference to your audience. And not just your own errors, but those of others as well.

Human nature seems to make us want to jump on every little mistake others make, perhaps in a desire to show our superiority. What good does that do? Social media seems to enhance this side of us and the pack mentality of the community can make us attack without mercy.

In May of 2015, sales at J. Crew dropped 10% over the previous year. Alejandro Rhett, Vice President of men's merchandising, delivered pink slips to some of the 175 employees who had been let go. Rhett was upset by the loss and went out with a few of his surviving colleagues for a drink. Unfortunately for him, he posted photos of himself and some of his colleagues on Instagram, complete with hashtags like these: #jcrewcrew, #gonegirl, #hungergames, #maytheoddsbeeverinyourfavor, #nofunhere.

The New York Post picked up the story and ran with it. Rhett took the photos down the next day, but not before the Post took screen grabs and shared them in an article.[25] J. Crew eventually fired Rhett, according to reports.

What's the lesson here? Never, ever use social media while under the influence of anything. No matter how smart or innocent it seems to you at that moment, it can change your life.

It should go without saying after reading this far in the book that you should be thoughtful about the person on the other end of the posts you share. How will it be received? Could it be misconstrued? If so, either don't share it or re-write it first. Consider your audience and your reputation.

According to a study by YouGov.com, 36% of respondents reported having regretted a social media post when they didn't properly consider a response. Sixteen percent said they most often made mistakes when they were busy and responded too quickly.

When an individual makes a mistake like this, they carry the brunt of the outrage from their audience. But when you make a mistake

---

[25] http://nypost.com/2015/06/17/j-crew-exec-brags-about-surviving-hunger-games-layoffs/

on a brand's social media presence, it looks bad for you, but perhaps worse for the company.

Hashtag jacking

Hashtags are a popular way to associate your message with a larger group of people. Alejandro Rhett was using the power of hashtags to express his emotions about the job cuts and referenced the movie 'Hunger Games', in which contestants fight to the death. Many brands have tried to leverage the popularity of hashtags to attract a larger audience. Hashtag jacking is when you use a hashtag that relates to your product or message in such a way that users of that hashtag are attracted to learn more or share the post with their social networks.

When the lights went out during the 2013 Superbowl, the team at Oreo jumped into action and posted what is now referred to in marketing circles as "The Oreo Moment". It was simply a Tweet: "Power out? No problem" and an image of an Oreo cookie on a darkened background with the words "You can still dunk in the dark". The Tweet was retweeted over 15,000 times and Twitter exploded. They didn't even use the hashtag for the game, but everyone else did.

PBS jumped onto the bandwagon too, with this tweet:

"This might be a good time to think about alternative programming. #SuperBowlBlackOut #WeHaveDowntonPBS"

These are both great examples of using hashtags to draw in an audience without seeming to "highjack" them. Unfortunately there are plenty of examples of thoughtless uses of hashtags for us to learn from.

DiGiorno Pizza

When a security video surfaced of NFL star Ray Rice in a hotel elevator punching his future wife, Janay Palmer, in the face and then dragging her unconscious body from the elevator, the video went viral.

Posts flooded social media networks and the news media as well. The two had now married, and people wondered why the now Mrs. Rice stayed with her abuser.

Domestic survivor and author Beverly Gooden created the hashtag #WhyIStayed to help people talk about why women stay with their abusers and the discussion around the tag was riveting. At last count there were over 50,000 mentions of the tag on social sites. Unfortunately, someone at DiGiorno Pizza saw that tag, and likely without realizing the context, Tweeted:

"#WhyIStayed You had pizza."

When they felt the backlash from Twitter, DiGiorno was quick to apologize:

"A million apologies. Did not read what the hashtag was about before posting."

Now, to be fair to DiGiornio, they are well known on Twitter to be quick-witted and popular for real time conversations with their users. They saw their mistake and corrected it as soon as possible. They even personally apologized to many of the people who complained about the fail on Twitter. Unfortunately, they are still known for "the DiGiorno fail".

MasterCard

A PR company representing MasterCard, a sponsor for the Brit Awards for Pop music, told journalists attending the event they could gain access only if they agreed to guarantee coverage of MasterCard in their social posts, right down to recommended Tweets, including the tag #PricelessSurprises, a link to somethingforthefans.co.uk, and the corporate username @MasterCardUK. The tweets needed to be shared before, during and after the event.

Many of the press attendees responded by outing the PR agency on Twitter, for example this one from Tim Walker:

"Please fellow journalists do not agree to the absurd conditions for covering @BRITAwards. I've even just been told what I should tweet. No."

It's not surprising the hashtag got hijacked by the press on this one. How do you think MasterCard and the Brit Awards responded to the PR agency?

While it's often frustrating for Marketing and PR to offer special event access, deals or other benefits to bloggers and press, realistic expectations must be set. In fact, by US law those tweets would have had to been accompanied by a disclosure of compensation in accordance with the FTC rules on endorsements.

Using hashtags

Always research hashtags before you use them. Do a search on the top platforms that use hashtags because tags are often used quite differently from platform to platform. Check the resources section of the website for links to hashtag tracking tools to help you see what people are saying.

If your hashtag does encounter an issue, you may decide to stop using it or think how you can turn it around. It is possible on occasion to take a hashtag back. The Mastercard tag #PricelessSurprises is still in use and seems to be doing quite well, but it may take a little time.

When you create a new tag, think about how it will be used long-term. Conferences often use the same tag year after year and append a date, like #16NTC for the Nonprofit Technology Conference. Think too about ways the tag could be misconstrued. Email it to some friends or members of your team to see what they think before you commit.

Hashtags are used differently on the various networks. Facebook and Twitter users rarely use more than one or two in a post but on Instagram it's common practice to use 5 or even 10. Check the network you're interested in and do some searches. See what other people are doing and then give it a little thought. Trust your gut. If a dozen hashtags feels like overload, it probably is.

Automated responses
Automation can be your friend, if used correctly. So can scripts given to the customer service people manning your social media accounts. It is important, though, not to over-automate or restrict customer service staff so much that a cut and paste reply is the best they can do. A thoughtful and authentic response that includes the necessary information is always preferred.

In June 2010, Matt Fischer's sister Katie was killed in a car accident. He posted his complaint about Progressive Insurance's handling of the case in a Tumblr blog post that was shared to Twitter among others. Progressive apparently had a response prepared and as the Tweets mentioning the post hit Twitter, they were responded to with a long Tweet (using TwitLonger) that said:

"This is a tragic case, and our sympathies go out to Mr. Fisher and his family for the pain they've had to endure. We fully investigated this claim and relevant background and feel we properly handled the claim within our contractual obligations. Again, this is a tragic situation, and we're sorry for everything Mr. Fisher and his family have gone through."

The tweets went out over and over on Progressive's Twitter feed, dominating the messaging. Four years later, Progressive settled with the family, but not after seeing quite a lot of negative PR on social and mass media.

Then there are the bots. Automated robots used for customer service can give a feeling of having been heard, and often are followed up by a real person. Not so in the case of Bank of America.

Mark Hamilton wrote an anti-foreclosure message on the sidewalk in front of a Manhattan Bank of America branch and was asked to leave by police.

He posted to Twitter:

"Just got chased away by #NYPD 4 'obstructing sidewalk."

Bank of America's account responded to him with:

"We'd be happy to review your account with you to discuss any concerns. Please let us know if you need assistance."

Then, as Mark's supporters started mentioning the incident, the Bank of America account responded to them with posts like:

"I work for Bank of America. What happened? Anything I can do to help? ^SA"

The messages alternated like this for quite some time, turning what might have been a conversation starter to resolve a customer issue into a customer relations nightmare.

Now, Bank of America says this was not a robot. They say it was a "social media service representative". If so, they need to give their service reps a little leeway in how they can respond to a request and a little training in listening.

While it seems more gaffs are made on Twitter (maybe because there is more of a sense of immediacy there) it's not just Twitter.

The Union Street Guest House
The Union Street Guest House in Hudson, New York was a popular venue for weddings and hotel staff were unhappy about some negative reviews posted by prior wedding guests on Yelp about the hotel. So, they posted a warning on their website for the happy couples, basically stating that if the guests at the wedding posted negative reviews about the hotel on Yelp, the hotel would bill the hosts $500 for each negative statement unless they were taken down.

"If your guests are looking for a Marriott type hotel they may not like it here. Therefore: If you have booked the Inn for a wedding or other type of event anywhere in the region and given us a deposit of any kind for guests to stay at USGH there will be a $500 fine that will be deducted from your deposit for every negative review of USGH placed on any internet site by anyone in your party and/or attending your wedding or event."

Again this was widely covered on social media and news services. Eventually, they removed the policy after Yelp stated it was against the spirit and policies of their site.

So what?
I could go on and on with examples like these, but that really isn't me being compassionate, kind or generous, now is it?

We humans love to watch someone else's mistakes, maybe because it could easily be our own dirty laundry on display. Instead, let's think about what we can learn from these lessons.

Be prepared
Everyone who uses social media should have a plan for how they interact on social media. Some of it is stupidly basic, and yet we still need to be told.

Never use social media under the influence of anything. Take a breath and re-read every post before you hit send.
If you are upset or conflicted about what to say, give it a little time before you send. Take a walk, breathe, give yourself time to respond in a thoughtful manner. Even if the situation that set you off was impulse-driven, your response doesn't have to be.

If you are using social media in a business situation, it is even more important to have a plan for both crisis management and day-to-day interaction. This is where having a social media policy can come in handy. The social policy document should outline what actions should be taken and who is responsible for taking necessary actions or for simply answering those hot button questions. There must be someone assigned to be in charge of damage control.

Many companies have a pre-written group of posts to send out in case of a crisis. This is great and can be very helpful, but as you can see in some of our cases, it can also be a disaster. Staff must know how to take that messaging and craft something authentic and appropriate. Rather than canned messages, I suggest using guidelines. If A happens then you should do B, etc.

Mistakes will happen. Never try to cover up a mistake. Trust me, that will simply make it all worse. Rather, own your mistakes. Be ready to acknowledge your humanity and to respond to people calling you out with a thoughtful response. Say thank you for bringing it you your attention. Tell them what action will be taken and follow through with that. If you aren't in a position to take action now, that's OK. Give them a timeline about when you'll get back to them.

Haters are gonna hate
We all get a little reactive when we're attacked, don't we? The fact is: haters are gonna hate. You can't help that. There are people in the world who are so miserable, they lash out just for the sake of lashing out, or to attract attention. I call them trolls. You know, they live under a bridge waiting for unsuspecting people to walk by and then pounce! Don't let the trolls draw you into their game.

Of course, not everyone who has a complaint is a troll. Train yourself and your team to step back for a moment. Is there validity in the comment? Is there an action you can take to resolve the issue? Can you respond with an authentic and helpful voice and turn the situation around?

Negative comments can be an opportunity to show that you listen to your users, and you care about what they have to say.

Thank commenters for their feedback and answer questions in a straightforward and honest manner.

If you don't know the answer, or it will take more than a simple response to a comment, say so and ask for a phone number or email address in a direct message (not in public) so you can follow up.

If there is a legitimate problem, thank them for bringing it to your attention and tell them how you will resolve it or that you've passed the issue along to the right person to resolve it.

If you have an on-line community or public Facebook page, post a link to your community guidelines clearly stating what kind of language and comments are acceptable and how they will be handled. If there are things such as hate speech, identity theft or spam that will get someone banned from the community, say so clearly. Refer to these guidelines when necessary and consider how to fine-tune the messaging to fit the situation rather than cutting and pasting a response.

****

Do this

Be sure you have a response plan in your social media policy so everyone knows how to respond in any scenario. Train everyone to give issues the attention they deserve and not to try to bury them or treat every complaint as negative. Have some written responses to common issues available but resist the urge to cut and paste a canned response.

Mindful Moment
Everyone deserves to be heard, and sometimes all you need to do is listen, recognize the value in what people have to say and let them know you care. Take the time to think before reacting or creating a social post you might regret.

CHAPTER ELEVEN

Pulling it all together

"Let's say someone rounded up all your content and placed it in a box, like it never existed. Would anyone miss it? Would you leave a gap in the marketplace?"
- Joe Pulizzi

Okay. So, now we understand the value of mindfulness. We understand a lot of things about how social media works and how we can set ourselves up for social media success. We understand how to learn from other people's mistakes and really make sure that we don't make them ourselves. We understand how to listen with intent instead of reacting to things, even though we want to respond to things immediately as they happen. We also understand a lot of ways that we can source content intelligently and use curation, as well as creating our own content.

Now, let's talk about how we're going to put it all to work on a day-to-day basis. It probably seems like you still have a lot of work to do, doesn't it? Well, yes, you do. But, if you are organized in how you do that work and you take a mindful and focused approach to getting it done, it won't be as hard as it might seem.

Let's get down to the nitty-gritty. Remember when we made a huge pile of all the content that we got from our team, outsourced, or curated? There is an enormous amount of content out there, and sometimes that gets in the way of us actually being able to put the steps in this book into practice to make that content useful.

Without a good plan and a content calendar, you could end up doing a lot of unnecessary extra work. I encourage you to download our sample content calendar from the website or create your own with a simple spreadsheet.

Look back at some of the ideas shared about content and remember the 80-20 rule: 80% of your content should be without a sales pitch or marketing message; 20% of your content can be driving sales or celebrating your successes. This is why curated content, conversation and sharing is so useful. Sort out the content you have and categorize it by platform, type, topic and the goal of sharing it. Then, you can start planning your content strategy around those different categories and getting a good mix of information and marketing.

Sometimes when I'm creating a content calendar for a client for the first time, we take large Post-it notes and write all of the topics that we can possibly think of, whether we have content for them or need to build content. Maybe it's new items or just events. You wouldn't believe the number of crazy events that go on in social media - Pickle Day, Pie Day, Pi Day, National Secretary Day, all of these other types of days that people celebrate. How can you do something for Bike to Work Day? Who could help but share content about Ice Cream Day? These dates are available on public calendars, and you can add them to your calendar.

Now, take all of those Post-it notes and put them on the wall. Organize them and see how they relate to each other. Or use a mind map like we did for Two Dog Leash. Once you put them all up there, you may start to see some themes. Group those themes together so that you can start to see what stories you have, what stories you need to build, and where you have holes that you need to fill. Now, remember that we want to focus on the 80-20 rule: 80% of the content that you post on social media should benefit people in a real way, and it should come from someone else or support someone else. Only 20% of what you put out there should be pitches. The first 80% may be educational, it may be news, it may be celebrating a holiday, it may be congratulating a colleague on a new job, or re-tweeting, or re-sharing information, even conversations.

Take Twitter or Facebook chats, Google Hangouts or live-stream video shows for example, there are a lot of things you can do that really fill up that 80%. Why the 80-20 rule? Social media is grounded by generosity and reciprocity. If you are generous in sharing my information, being kind to me, and creating a relationship, we develop trust with each other. I am very happy to share your information because now I trust you, I like you, and I think that your mission probably aligns with mine. When you're putting it all to work and you're trying to decide how you're going to schedule things across your day, you always want to think about that 80-20 rule and keep that idea of generosity in the back of your mind.

You want to bring your community into your online discussion. Enable them to feel confident about knowing you as a resource. Enable them to feel powerful because they have someone from whom they can gather information and then share with their networks, which makes them look good. Both of those things will make them feel positively toward you. This isn't a manipulative kind of thing, it's really basic to any conversation. There has to be a give and take, there has to be a level of generosity, there has to be a level of trust.

Maybe you won't do all of this yourself. Lots of times, the marketing team is small, and they don't have enough resources to do everything. You need to find out who on your team can help you and assign someone, if nothing else, to collate all the proposed content. Once they bring it together, it will be easier to put it out there, or to give to an agency or consultant to execute for you.

If you want your employees to help with this, you can enable them with a social media kit and maybe even some training so that they understand what it is that you need them to do. They should have a central area where files, images, and messaging are contained. If they want to share some of your success stories, that's great!

Make sure that your employees know where the logo is. Make sure they know where photos of the founder are located. If you create a fantastic infographic for your business, send it out to your entire team by e-mail and ask them to share it on social media with their own comments. This is one way to really expand your reach and be the central connection point within your own company. Again, you're enabling your staff to be stronger and more intelligent within their own social networks. We're not asking them to sell for us, we're asking them to share information. This is a way for them to garner thought leadership as well.

Talk to your team. Find out who your advocates are, who has a really strong voice, who's really active on social media. See how they can help you to put your social strategy to work day by day.

Set some guidelines in a corporate social media policy

One of the things that we always recommend for an organization, no matter how small, is to set up some guidelines for how social media is to be used related to the business. You want to make sure of some basics.

I talked about social media policies in Chapter 3 and there are several resources on the website that give you great examples from companies like IBM and the Red Cross, who have particularly excellent social media policies for their staff. Take a look at those and see how you can pull one together for yourself. If you need help putting together a social media policy, contact me through the website and I will gladly discuss how we can help you do that.

Train, if necessary

Training may not be necessary for all of your staff. However, you may find that you have some people who are natural mavens, but don't use the social media networks that you would like help with. If that happens, you can decide if you're going to train them on how to use those different networks. You may want to have in-house training. Have someone come in and spend half the day with the staff to help them understand the value of social media and some of the things that we've covered in this book.

You may also want to train them on how to use various tools that you have set up for your company. For example, you might be using Sprout Social or Hootsuite as a communications tool. If so, you're going to want to make sure your employees are trained in at least the basics of how to use that tool.

Organization is your friend with social media. The more organized you are, the more content you can deliver, the better your quality will be, and the less time you'll spend on managing the tools. You'll actually spend more time working and that's a good thing, isn't it? But, a little too much organization may feel rigid, and it may be difficult to really get conversations going, especially if you over-automate. If your automation tools are sending out a lot of messages but you don't take the time or have the time to respond to the messages you get, it's a total waste. Try not to let that happen to you.

Remember to occasionally drop into your social media accounts and leave a little room for serendipity. Serendipity may seem like a silly idea, but it really does work. If you scan your social media accounts maybe two or three times a day for 5 minutes and simply respond to things that you find there, you will start to have conversations that may be a little bit out of your sphere and introduce you to new people. So, don't forget to spend some unscheduled time online and be generous in how you communicate with people.

****

Do this

Interview your team and find the evangelists. Decide if they need training, or if they are people that you want to interview and have someone else write for them. Hold a brainstorming session for content topics and plan a regular meeting to keep the ball rolling and everyone engaged. Be absolutely sure that you share your triumphs in social media with your entire team. Celebrate the people who have had great successes and let everyone know that they're doing an excellent job. This brings everyone to the table happy and focused.

Mindful moment

We often forget how smart our team is, since we see them every day. Take a moment to be mindful of them and all they have to offer. Appreciate them and let them help you all be successful together.

CHAPTER TWELVE

Resources

"Today, knowledge has power. It controls access to opportunity and advancement."
- Peter Drucker

There have been quite a few resources shared throughout this book and I list them below, chapter by chapter. If you are reading the e-book version, you can click on these titles and they will go to the websites with the reference. But, if you're reading it in print or listening to the audio book, just go to the website MindfulSocialMarketing.com/resources and you'll find these links and many more there.

Social media is constantly changing and adapting to the needs of the users—which is one of my great joys—so I've held back from being too specific about networks and tools here. Rather, look to the website for current information. I've created several lists and I'll add to these lists as new tools and resources become available.

I love discovering new things and sharing them and this website gives me an opportunity to do just that.

I will be offering training and classes on the website as well as these free resources, so stay tuned!

You can connect with me through the newsletter and blog on MindfulSocialMarketing.com, as well as at:

JanetFouts.com

TatuDigital.com

Twitter: http://twitter.com/jfouts

Facebook: http://facebook.com/jfouts

Linkedin: http://linkedin.com/in/janetfots

about.me/jfouts

Email: janet@janetfouts.com

Phone: 408.216.7423

Believe it or not, the best way to reach me is through a direct message on Twitter or maybe a phone call.

Chapter 1

The non-discriminating heart: loving kindness meditation training decreases implicit intergroup bias. http://j.mp/1MAIZqE

Loving-kindness meditation increases social connectedness. - PubMed - NCBI http://j.mp/1j1zap5

Meditation-based treatment yielding immediate relief for meditation-naïve migraineurs. http://j.mp/1iHK17I

Chapel Hill study (PDF) http://j.mp/1KEV9MO

Association of an Educational Program in Mindful Communication With Burnout, Empathy, and Attitudes Among Primary Care Physicians http://j.mp/1KZZTP8

Mindfulness Stress Reduction And Healing http://j.mp/1JjMwlq

Association of an Educational Program in Mindful Communication With Burnout, Empathy, and Attitudes Among Primary Care Physicians http://j.mp/1KZZTP8

The Pomodoro Technique http://j.mp/1Qs3cN4

Facebook Compassion Research Day https://www.facebook.com/compassion

Chapter 2

Acquity Group study on buyer's research habits http://j.mp/1Ktc5m9

Elite Daily Millennial Study 2015 http://j.mp/1iHODut

Chapter 3

Intel's social media policy http://j.mp/1ir9txy

Chapter 5

Now This https://nowthisnews.com/

DataMinr https://www.dataminr.com/

Pat Roberts video "Just Let it Go" https://youtu.be/xU4NJS-Yum4

Pat Robert's tweet #forthegrandkids
https://twitter.com/senpatroberts/status/588752993425739776

CrowdTangle listening tool http://www.crowdtangle.com/

Chapter 6

Jay Baer, Youtility http://j.mp/1NXStwC

Chapter 7

FTC Guidelines on ads and disclosure
https://www.ftc.gov/sites/default/files/attachments/press-
releases/ftc-staff-revises-online-advertising-disclosure-
guidelines/130312dotcomdisclosures.pdf

Chapter 8

JD Power benchmark study on social CRM
http://www.jdpower.com/press-releases/2013-social-media-
benchmark-study

Chapter 10

J Crew article in the New York Post
http://nypost.com/2015/06/17/j-crew-exec-brags-about-
surviving-hunger-games-layoffs/

YouGov.com
https://today.yougov.com/news/2015/07/22/social-media-
blunders-cause-more-damage-important-/

The Oreo Tweet
https://twitter.com/oreo/status/298246571718483968

Acknowledgments

There are so many who have helped me over the years. Here are some books and resources from my mentors and people mentioned in this book.

Books to read

The Organized Mind: Thinking Straight in the Age of Information Overload: Daniel J. Levitin: http://j.mp/1OJMwT5

Mindful Work, David Gelles http://j.mp/1Ml6Do7

Focus: The Hidden Driver of Excellence, Daniel Goleman http://j.mp/1YsRZSv

Real Happiness at Work: Meditations for Accomplishment, Achievement, and Peace, Sharon Salzberg http://j.mp/1OoBEut

Ted Rubin on #RonR http://j.mp/1V4xDKN

Shareology: How Sharing is Powering the Human Economy http://j.mp/1L3BZx3

18 Minutes- Find Your Focus, Master Distraction and Get the Right Things Done http://j.mp/1LqU3oH

Human to Human http://j.mp/1j2e1e5

Youtility http://j.mp/1NXStwC

Epic Content Marketing http://j.mp/1OhsYF3

People mentioned in the book

Jon Kabat-Zinn
Scientist, writer, and meditation teacher
http://twitter.com/jonkabatzinn

Loic Le Meur
Co-Founder of LeWeb and 5 other startups
http://twitter.com/loic

Evan Williams
Passionate Photographer - Chief Adventurist
http://twitter.com/Ev

Arianna Huffington
Co-Founder and Editor-in-Chief
http://twitter.com/AriannaHuffingt

Daniel Levitin
Author
http://twitter.com/danlevitin

Daniel Goleman
Author
http://twitter.com/DanielGolemanEI

LivaJudic
http://twitter.com/LivaJudic

Patagonia
Clothing company
http://twitter.com/patagonia
Casey Sheahan
http://twitter.com/CaseySheahan1

Peter Deng
Appreciator of Craft, Director
http://twitter.com/pxd

David Gelles
Author
http://twitter.com/dgelles

Sharon Salzberg
Meditation Teacher & Author
http://twitter.com/SharonSalzberg

Seth Godin
Author, blogger
http://twitter.com/ThisIsSethsBlog

Ted Rubin
http://twitter.com/TedRubin

Neal Schaffer
Author, Founder
http://twitter.com/NealSchaffer

Peter Bregman
Author
http://twitter.com/peterbregman

SproutSocial
Social media management
http://twitter.com/SproutSocial

Congressman Pat Roberts
http://twitter.com/PatRoberts

Bryan Kramer
CEO PureMatter
http://twitter.com/bryankramer

Jay Baer
Author
http://twitter.com/jaybaer

Jason Falls
Author
http://twitter.com/JasonFalls

JoePulizzi
http://twitter.com/JoePulizzi

Johndeere (the tractor company)
http://twitter.com/JohnDeere

Frank Strong
http://twitter.com/Frank_Strong

Jill Rowley
Startup Advisor. Keynote Speaker
http://twitter.com/jill_rowley

Danzarella
Social Media Scientist
http://twitter.com/danzarrella

Joel Comm
Author
http://twitter.com/joelcomm

Guy Kawasaki
Chief evangelist
http://twitter.com/GuyKawasaki

Zappos
http://twitter.com/zappos

Bill Gates
http://twitter.com/BillGates

Beverly Gooden
Creator, domestic violence expositor, speaker
http://twitter.com/bevtgooden

Tim Walker
Author
http://twitter.com/timwalker

Mark Hamilton
Journalism instructor
http://twitter.com/darthmarkh

Kare Anderson
Emmy-winner, TED speaker
http://twitter.com/KareAnderson

Courtney Smith
Co-founder/executive creative director
http://twitter.com/cshasarrived

About the Author

Janet Fouts is CEO and principal strategist at Tatu Digital Media, a social media marketing agency in Silicon Valley serving brands from social good organizations like Human Journey (co-founded by Archbishop Desmond Tutu) to tech startups and Fortune 500 corporations.

As a corporate trainer on digital marketing and mindfulness, Janet conducts seminars around the world on making mindful social media an integral part of a successful marketing program.

She keynotes and leads seminars at conferences around the world making social media approachable with actionable tips attendees can put right to use.

Janet is listed as one of the top 50 Marketing Thought Leaders Over 50 by Brand Quarterly Magazine and the Top 100 Giving Influencers on Twitter by Give Local America. She is frequently quoted in the press, including USA Today, Forbes Magazine, and Thought Leader Life. When she's not working, she's spending time with friends and family or riding her horse in the foothills of the Santa Cruz mountains.

CPSIA information can be obtained
at www.ICGtesting.com
Printed in the USA
BVHW042101110119
537631BV00015B/715/P

9 781495 190322